The White Picket Fence

Crown for Life Pursues Biblical Boundaries

KATHLEEN DERBYSHIRE

ENDORSEMENTS

In the parable of the Great Supper Luke 14:23, Jesus gives directions to go out into the highways and hedges and compel them to come in, that my house may be filled. This book not only compels them to come in, but walks along beside them through their journey to wholeness. Building fences leads and guides those who have allowed compulsions and lackadaisical behaviour to overtake their position in Christ. With determination, sheer resolve, learning about oneself and awareness of your habits, allows answers and successes to be obtained by the reading of God's Word, creating boundaries and by being led by the Holy Spirit.

Rev. Della Bost,
Pastor of First Baptist Church, Puce, Ontario

In her book The White Picket Fence, Kathleen V. Derbyshire brings her readers into the lives of several women and their counselors as they look to overcome habitual issues in their lives. The author is able to use her novella to entertain her readers and to also teach them of key Biblical foundations in overcoming sin that have taken root in our lives. The White Picket Fence workshop would be beneficial to churches and individuals in all stages of their Christian walk.

Rev. Dale S Sanger MTS, B.Th
Lead Pastor, New Life Assembly, Belle River, Ontario

THE PICKET WHITE FENCE

Copyright © 2017 Kathleen Derbyshire

All rights reserved.

ISBN: 1977677800
ISBN-13: 978-1977677808

Printed in Canada
Windsor, Ontario

Cover design by Derek Ouellette

Editor McKenzie Spies, Gold Raven Editing

Publishing service provided by

In conjunction with Createspace.com. Visit AuthorsBestFriend.ca for details.

CONTENTS

	Acknowledgments	i
1	In the Beginning	1
2	Become Aware	10
3	What Sparks a Fire	21
4	Allowing Intervention	33
5	Wisdom Behind Knowing	48
6	Fortify Yourself	64
7	Encourage and Inspire	79
8	The Power of Change	95
9	Your Turn Now	107
	About the Author	124

ACKNOWLEDGMENTS

I want to thank my Lord and Saviour Jesus Christ for every word that is on every page of this book. He has given me every gift I utilized to write this book and every Biblical life skill I have employed to live an abundant life. I am honoured to follow Him.

I would also like to thank my friend Jennifer Walker for working with me for months editing the content of this book to make it as wonderful as it has turned out to be.

A big thank you also goes out to my mom, Betty-Jean McIntyre, for her support and encouragement during this time. She continuously reminded me of my talent every step of the way.

1
IN THE BEGINNING

If not for years of struggle, victory would not be mine. If not for ungodly traps and being deceived by people, I would not have gone on a search for the truth. This search for the truth has made me who I am today. This is my first thought as I admire the country cottage birdfeeder hanging outside the window. It is teaming with early risers. I love to sit at my desk, watching them flutter around. I am the early bird in this place. I brew coffee and spend some alone time with Jesus before the day slips right out of my hands. My desk is my favourite place to drink coffee, not looking at anything but seeing everything, not thinking about anything but thinking about everything. Jesus is always on my mind, and so are women. This is the reason for this desk, this office, and this time.

I still think about the past and how I came to be who I am now, The Biblical Life Skills Strategist. I don't remember what my parents taught me, growing up, about life, but whatever it was, it took up wings and flew out of my head. As much as I search my mind I cannot locate even a morsel of what my teachers taught, because it apparently was eaten by those same birds that took my parents' teachings too. In spite of all the missing knowledge, I yearned to have a good life. I didn't know what a good life was, but I did know I wasn't living it then. I was falling apart and I knew it. My emotional roller-coaster rides and non-existent financial aptitude were proof of it. Surely there has to be a better way to live than this? When I began asking myself this question, and seeking out the answer, my life began to change, and Jesus allowed me to see Him.

He had been there all along, drawing me to Him. I discovered He knew me before I was born and named me before the creation of the Earth.[1] He chose me, Leola Lurned. Leola means lion. I pursued Him and the abundant life He so graciously offered me like a lion. I am living it now as a result of years of being taught by Jesus what my good life looks like from His eyes. Through His eyes is how I see everything. He showed me when He called me His that I would teach women what He has taught me. I smile, on this day, remembering how long ago it was and the painful but productive journey it turned out to be. He is working out everything He told me from years ago up until this very day. It was a process to understand everything I am using to teach today. Every bit of information He gave me I pondered and worked out in my life. I asked the hard questions, knowing the answers would hurt but heal my broken heart.

I asked 'why', which led me to a need to know why I was the way I was, to make it easier for me to change. I started with my childhood and worked my way to my adult self. I was raised during the time when women were burning their bras. Women's liberation was beginning to flourish and so was role confusion. Going through these times was tough on everyone, especially the kids. Some women burned their bras, refusing to be traditional wives and mothers in order to make their way in the workforce. Some women burned only half of their bras and went out into the workforce with the commendable idea they can make the bacon and have plenty

---

[1] Psalm 139:1-24

of time to serve it up, all while being the perfect wife and mother too. Other women went out into the workforce to replace men rather than work with them. I have seen all three of these types of women in my adult work life. Which one of these 'free to be me' women would be me? I could be all of them. Becoming a single parent in my mid-twenties defined exactly who I would be. I would be the provider for my kids, their mother and their father.

Those days as a child were spent frolicking without a care in the world. How I could ever have thought as an adult I would have a good life, with absolutely no training, was beyond me. Then, to my dismay, I raised my own children with the same mindset, because I couldn't train them to know what I did not know myself. Now, I am watching my grandchildren being raised the same way and praying the craziness ends, knowing it won't, because doing the same thing over and over expecting different results each time is crazy. This is a mistake I cannot fix, because it is a generation away from being my business. I am responsible for three generations of craziness, yet I know I can only change myself; when I realized this, that is when the change began to happen. The craziness in my life stopped when Jesus Christ changed who I saw myself to be. He taught me, despite every era before and after, that the best knowledge about life could only be found in the Word of God. In there is the truth about life. It is the Book of Life, so I soaked it all up and found the good life or, rather, it found me.

In this search, the stories I told myself that made me vulnerable to deception were exposed, and I discovered the Truth that makes me free.[2] He has taught me this so thoroughly today that I rely on Him for every major decision I make. Jesus Christ is the only One who has been able to set me free from the lies that led me into the sins I got caught up in, robbing me of the good life. I can give credit to no one but Him for the transformation in my life, and I know He

---

[2] John 8:32

will transform the lives of the women in my area, so I work for Him to do just that.

As I sip my coffee, I remember from His Word the reasons He came for me and for every woman. *I have come that they may have life, and that they may have it more abundantly.*[3] He has placed in me a passion for women and has sent me to show them His way to an abundant life through His Word. I believe everything He says in His Word. The abundant life He has is available to all women if we could just get the skills we use to live under control. I was in my mid-thirties when I asked the freeing question, "How can I have a better life?"

Nearly ten years later, in my early forties, He called me to be part of the church. At that time, I was unruly, ungoverned, and uneducated in the school of life, but all the things I was doing to undo myself He would use to put me back together. He began tearing down the old me and building up the new Leola. As painful as it was, I went with Him. For many years I fumbled around, wrestled with God, and despised myself before the good life began. I sit in my office today a free woman whose heart has been healed by the only One who can do it, Jesus Christ. I offer Him, and only Him, as the way to the good life. How wonderful it will be to see women benefit from my growth under the wings of Jesus. His plan for them is great. His plan for me is great, and I thank God I will not be alone.

Occupying the desk beside me is a woman God has raised up, whose passion for women is as grand as mine. Veronica and I have become fast friends, sharing everything with each other, including God's plan for each of us. We have been amazed by everything God has accomplished in our lives so far. When God revealed His plan for me, I begged Him to allow me to have a partner. God answered my prayer in the form of Veronica Keene. I was excited for Veronica's arrival into my life, but patience was called for to see what God had planned. Veronica and I have studied God's Word together

---

[3] John 10:10

for many years. He made both of us ready for this adventure together, and we are excited about the message He has laid on our hearts to relay. We know helping women will be a daunting task, because we know how hard it was for Jesus Christ to help us through our insecurities and shame. God has made us both strong in Him first, and strong in our knowledge of Him.

Since God has brought the concept of life skills to my attention, He has opened my eyes to all of the issues to plague us with money, people, truth, and the like. No matter where we are or where we go, we will come across many people who lack the skills to improve their lives. Women definitely need to help each other by supporting each other through developing Biblical life skills. When I began changing my life skills into the Biblical life skills God gave me, I found out what good living is all about. I began to see life through the eyes of Jesus, and it looked good to me. My work did not depend on what others said, it was dependent on what Jesus said.

I remember, as I take another sip of coffee, how many times I asked for a miracle from God to just 'be changed', but He denied my request. Without that time to develop Biblical life skills, I would not have the strength to overcome the perilous times I was to go through under His guidance. I began to write and teach life skills workshops to women in 2005, to teach what I was learning about change. Those workshops would be the beginning of our journey to teach women the great power in being an overcomer with Jesus. Veronica and I would reach out to women who were in need of "Overcomer Training" to discover God's way for them to have the abundant life in Jesus Christ. We knew this would be difficult because we are in the perilous last days according to God's Word.

Based on all the knowledge God has given me, I believe Him when He says, *in the last days perilous times shall come* (2 Timothy 3:1), in which people will be lovers of themselves and, as a result, *this sort are those who creep into households and make captives of gullible women loaded down with sins, led away by various lusts, always learning and never able to come to the knowledge of the truth* (2 Timothy 3:6-7). The fact that this sort is coming after women in the last days has broken both of our hearts for what breaks the heart of Jesus. We praise our God, however, for those who have been able to stand their ground to be victorious in getting the blessing the Lord has promised every one of us who love Him – the crown of life.

Blessed is the man who endures temptation; for when he has been approved, he will receive the crown of life, which the Lord has promised to those who love Him (James 1:12). To be an overcomer is to be blessed by God. Satan does not want to see us endure or overcome his temptations to get that crown of life. I furrowed my forehead and thought, "I don't care if Satan wants me to have that crown or not, Jesus says I can have that crown if I endure temptation. I am going to do everything I can to get that crown *and* I am going to help every woman, who will let me, get that crown too." I smile and nod, hoping the devil is looking.

I am still in awe over how much my life has changed since Jesus Christ tamed me. The reality of it makes me cry every time I think of it. With my Bible opened in front of me, I ask God, "Why did you choose me?" His instant answer, "Why not you?" This answer reassures me, and I continue to marvel over how this all came into being and what I am committed to do. I never want to forget where I came from, because it is from there that here became possible.

Veronica and I have talked over our goal many times to make sure we are clear about whom we are and what we provide. To provide the "Overcomer Training" we use, we will spend our lives searching God's Word to lead women on their journey to *His* way toward the abundant life. God says in His Word *[for] no temptation has overtaken you except such as is common to man; but God is faithful, who will not allow you to be tempted beyond what you are able, but with the temptation will also make the way of escape, that you may be able to bear it* (1 Corinthians 10:13). Just as *each one is tempted when he is drawn away by his own desires and enticed. Then, when desire has conceived, it gives birth to sin; and sin, when it is full-grown, brings forth death* (James 1:14-15). Satan and the world present giving into our temptation as the good life. We give in to that which we believe will be a pleasure. Eventually we become exhausted from working hard to maintain that pleasure. Soon, the enjoyment of the pleasurable life wears off, and we become its slave. I walked this path many times until I saw how taxing it really was daily. I began to say "no" to temptation, but had no power behind my "no", and fell right back into slavery. In my slavery, God taught me the power behind having Biblical boundaries. There is no reason why I cannot put a fence around me to protect myself and, since I love white picket fences, those are exactly what I put around myself. I smiled at the memory. I am such a visual person. How much my life began to change when I began standing behind God's Word to me. When He told me to stop doing something, I went about learning what the best way to do that was, and I did it. Every woman can do the same.

Women can overcome temptation to receive the crown of life by becoming *faithful until death to receive the crown of life* (Revelation 2:10). *Now faith is the substance of things hoped for, the evidence of things not seen* (Hebrews 11:1), but *he who comes to God must believe that He is, and that He is a rewarder of those who diligently seek Him* (Hebrews 11:6). If God rewards us with the crown of life for enduring temptation and being faithful, then our goal in this life should be that crown. I am devoted to showing women the way to Jesus as He shows them the escape from their temptation. The crown of life is waiting for us on the other side of the very first time we endure temptation to earn it, and it will be on our head for life. I see myself every day wearing the crown of life. When Veronica and I were pondering a name for our newly formed alliance, I told her about the crown I see on my head every day and how I wished all women could see the crown for their whole life. "Crown for Life" became our name and we love it. It has become our motto as well – 'Let us lead you to Jesus Christ, so you too can overcome to get the crown for life.'

We want "Crown for Life" to be a place women can come to explore God's way to the abundant life through developing strategic Biblical life skills to live a good life. Together, we are the Biblical Life Skills Strategists. We strategize with God, each other, and our clients to show them how to escape the chains that hold them in slavery. Living a good life is our goal, and we want it to be theirs too, but none of this is possible without Jesus Christ; therefore, leading women to Him is our number one priority.

I laughed to think about how we struggled even opening the business. Veronica and I were working out of my basement for a little while when God called us to rent an office. Veronica, who has a head for finances, looked at me, shocked: "Our last three pro-bono cases did not do anything for our bank account, therefore we are strapped for cash. How will we pay rent if our bank account goes empty every month?" She was fit to be tied when I suggested we rent a new place. It wasn't that my house wasn't good, but Sam, my husband, is very uncomfortable with people coming into his personal space. I had been praying about it but hadn't said anything to Veronica. Sam loves Veronica, but he wants her out of his personal space. I asked her to pray about it.

She came back the next day and said God had spoken to her, and He informed her we are to move. I marveled about how quickly God spoke to her, and I was so proud of her that she listened even though she is uptight about money. "I do not see how we are going to find a place to rent in this area for as cheap as this place." She smiled one of those quirky smiles she has when she is fooling with me.

"Well, I think we ought to let God take care of that and just do our part to find it." I smiled at her, knowing she was trying not to worry. We were not used to depending on God for absolutely everything yet, because we had been depending on our own resources to minister to women thus far. Finding a place to rent and doling out money we didn't have was going to be a bit of a struggle, even for me.

I looked around and said, "You did right by us, Jesus, with this office, and we will do right by you in believing you will provide everything."

2
BECOME AWARE

Crown for Life is located in a two-story house completely converted to office space on Huron Church Line. We border LaSalle and Windsor in Ontario, Canada. Our landlord lives next door and keeps the office looking like a well-manicured home. Robert and Dorothy MacIntyre are followers of Jesus Christ who were intrigued by our goals for women in the Body of Christ, so they rented this office to us, regardless of the many other lucrative offers they had received. Due to the bidding wars on real estate in our area, low cost houses and offices are hard to find. We had rescinded our offer on this office after great discussions about finances. We provide unpaid services as well as paid services that leave us in a position of financial need sometimes. God has always provided, but we did not want to push our blessings with Him. We explained the complexity of it to our landlord and exited the bidding process with heavy hearts. Two days later, to our complete surprise, he gave us the keys, and here we are today. If we were not sure before, we are now, that we are following the plan of God for this business. We love our office and we love our work; what else could we ask for, except maybe a normal neighbourhood in which to work.

After one week in our new office we have developed a system based on our arrival times. I am specializing in brewing the morning coffee, heating the office, and bringing in the newspaper, while Veronica takes out the trash at night, turns off the lights, and sets the alarm. Since this was formerly an apartment, we opted to keep the refrigerator and stove so we can make our lunch each day right inside the office. Along with dishes, we brought a microwave. It is like going from home to home again, although we did opt, with reluctance, to wear dress casual rather than our pajamas. We know if we allowed ourselves to wear pajamas we would not leave the office and our families might miss us. With a second cup of coffee in hand, I went back to my desk to pray over the day and continue to watch the birds. I was pondering how to handle our next set of overcomer trainees. In the past, God had brought women to us with hurdles in common, and this time it seemed He had done it again.

Before I can get to my desk with my coffee, I hear someone slowly walking up the steps, a bark, then running. The door flew open, and Veronica burst in with her hands full of office supplies, gasping for air. She is about five feet five inches tall, with shoulder length brown hair perfectly parted on the side, never out of place. My first thought when I saw her come in was, "She is not going to be a happy camper about how her hair looks right now." My second was, "Whose dog is that?" A black dog, almost as tall as Veronica, came straight at me, barking and wagging its tail. With no time to waste, I steeled myself for the impact. The dog was attempting to stop but, with the wood floors, the dog slid its way right into my legs and knocked me backwards into my chair. The dog jumped up on my lap and licked my face until it saw coffee all over the desk and began to lick that instead. The dog had a huge tongue that had tasted both my face and my coffee before I even had a chance to get back to my desk.

"Margaret Thatcher." The figure in the doorway bellowed.

Up until this second, Veronica had impressively been able to balance her load, but the voice from behind her was the final straw. All her supplies hit the floor when she jumped with alarm. Unhampered by any falling objects, the dog hightailed it through the objects to the man in the door, circled him and sat beside him, looking up into his eyes. I stopped staring at the man long enough to see the huge mess on my desk and now the floor. Our canine visitor had caused chaos in our office, but since she was a dog, her master would front the blame. Before I spoke a word, my "intuitive antenna" went up and I decided to keep my mouth shut. I have been known to speak before my brain is loaded and shoot myself in the foot. I plastered my tongue to the roof of my mouth in anticipation this guy had a good explanation.

"I do apologize for Marg's invasion of your barracks. She has taken it upon herself to be the welcoming committee for all the new neighbours," the man in the door said. "She is a retired police dog who still feels the need to police the neighbourhood. I will help you clean up." He looked at Margaret Thatcher. "Stay," he said, and she did.

It only took a few minutes to clean up. Henry, the man in the door, excused himself after everything was back in place. On his way down the stairs he yelled, "Come." Margaret Thatcher, who had stayed in the same spot she was ordered to stay in, left like a bolt of lighting and followed her master down the stairs. According to her master, Henry, she waits until she thinks the neighbour is fully moved in and comfortable, then she gets excited to meet them. She must have sensed we were making ourselves at home because she picked today to visit. I think Marg is right – we are comfortable here in this office, in this neighbourhood.

Veronica put all of her supplies away and filled her cup with a well-deserved coffee. She looked through the files I created laying on her desk. Thankfully, we are both very organized yet gifted in different ways for completing our tasks. Veronica is good at asking questions and listening, so she does all the intake meetings. I go through the notes to see if there are any more questions we need answered and create the file folders. Once that is complete, we come together to pray for them and discuss what "Overcomer Tool" we can use or develop. If we do not have this scenario already covered, we will create a new tool. The skill we desire most from God is to discern the root cause of each of their particular problematic situations. What do they not know that they could learn to modify this situation in their life? We have had four women visit us in this past week, with similar but different scenarios God has called them to modify. We know from experience the root issue is the same, so we are going through each file, searching for key things to lead us to the one thing we need, God's directive.

Once Veronica is settled, we begin our morning ritual asking our Lord to supply us with wisdom and understanding, so His people would be able to find their way to Him and find their way to the abundant life in Him. We ask Him for guidance to find the perfect Scripture to determine the link, for the wisdom to discuss these situations with love and affection for each other and for our clients.

Veronica and I are not your typical prayer warriors, which means praying before we start has to be God working in us, because it certainly would not be our first line of defense. Both of our minds go into our own problem-solving mode before we ask God to show us the solution. We know some prayer warriors who pray constantly, so we requested prayer for our business and our clients. Even our landlord's wife, Dory, is praying for us. We opened this business to help the body of Christ, but we know the body of Christ will not be helped without seeking the Lord first. We must talk to Jesus constantly,[4] so when we give our instructions to our clients they can trust we are giving them the Biblical way to improve their life skills and not our way. Both of us are susceptible to putting our own two cents in therefore we are each other's accountability partners. Each "Overcomer Tool" must be sifted through the Scriptures to make sure it agrees

---

[4] 1 Thessalonians 5:17

with the Word of God. If it does not line up with Scripture, it will not be fruitful for our clients.

We are both stunned by how many clients have come to Crown for Life this past week. We prayed about how to advertise, because word of mouth was not enough to pay our rent anymore. Last week, our first week in our new office, we had four new women seek our help. As I was staring out the window, thinking about how God had provided for us, I was wondering how we were going to provide for them, because, as of this moment, we had not found the link we know is there. I was just thinking we would need to work individually when I saw Veronica get up and begin dancing around her desk. She has a not-so subtle way of displaying her victories, although, honestly, I think she has no idea she is even doing it. She is just celebrating her victory; however, I call it the "Deskie Dance." I create new names for things I cannot describe with more than two words. Age has given me a great ability to forget, but I never forget the quirky names I flippantly give things. When she got around her desk to face me, she smiled with teeth so white and straight I was blinded. She said, "I've got it! I found the link." and returned to her deskie dance.

Relieved, I said with great excitement, "That is fantastic! What is it?"

"Matthew 5:37. Thank you, Jesus. Thank you, Jesus, for computer search engines." She sang while she continued to dance. I grabbed my favourite Bible, which never got one drop of coffee on it, miraculously. I have never seen Veronica display this side of herself with a client in the room, so I suspect she uses her "intuitive antenna" before she breaks out into those moves. She would not be a good candidate for *Dancing With the Stars*, but I love watching her moves.

"Matthew 5:37," I read, *"But let your 'Yes' be 'Yes,' and your 'No,' 'No.' For whatever is more than these is from the evil one."* I locate her in her dance path, "By Job, I think you've got it," I said with my best British accent. With a little more researching, I discover another verse just like it in James.[5] I believe this to be confirmation from God. Now, linking this directive with other verses toward this new theory will be our task.

In our initial visit with these four clients, they expressed concerns about not being able to stop themselves from doing specific things each day, no matter how hard they have tried. Our clients have a range of issues falling under the description found in this verse. We discussed this verse at length after Veronica's dance was complete. We became interested in the reason Jesus spoke this directive. He was on the mount beside the Sea of Galilee when He told His followers not to make vows they were sure to break. He wanted them to stop swearing their oaths on heaven or earth, just follow through with what they spoke.[6] He did not tell us how to do this, but just to do it. Jesus is well-aware we lack self-control. Our flesh will lead us astray in a second if we do not set our mind to take control of it. Herein lies the problem. We swear our oaths, knowing they are not worth the weight of the words we used to swear them. We may not do it meaning to break them, but we do.

The power we are given by the Holy Spirit is stronger than our sin of breaking oaths. Should we follow the Holy Spirit of God, we would not break an oath because we would not swear an oath. We would simply do what we say. If we give Jesus the control He requires, we will be victorious over every sin, but too often we plow our own path to where God requires us to be. Our path typically leads us to many things we did not intend, resulting in "the backtrack". We all know about "the backtrack". As a result of backtracking, it is harder to clean up the rotting wood around us than it was to make it. We get comfortable in the rotting wood until God tells us to rebuild. This is currently where our new clients are. They have been told to rebuild, but they are missing the hammer.

---

[5] James 5:12
[6] Matthew 5:34-36

God has given Veronica and I great success with examining His Word to find the tools needed, based on our own history and the Biblical characters' histories. In the past, I have asked God questions about current events in my life, only to find the answer in a story of one of the characters He has pointed me toward. We are also given insight into how Jesus intends for them to find their way out of their sins into His righteous way. The fact that Matthew 5:37 and James 5:12 are the perfect verses to describe our latest group of issues tells us only one thing: These women have a common problem that afflicts all of us. They say "yes" when they should say "no", and say "no" when they should say "yes". Based on what the Lord has revealed to us, the direction we need to go is to teach our new clients how to set Biblical boundaries for themselves and defend them. In my past teachings about boundaries, I have equated having boundaries to being surrounded by a "White Picket Fence". In those teachings, we discussed the need for the fence to have a foundation with sturdy posts. We also discussed how having no or few boundaries causes the fence to be unstable. I am a visual person who teaches with visual aids, and I see no need to veer from that path.

Veronica and I got right to work discerning how Jesus would have them build their fences. I was writing on the "mile long whiteboard" we had on the wall in the office, while Veronica furiously typed on the computer. The board was filled with arrows, words, Scripture, and ideas. I took a picture of it and rubbed it off to continue our discussion. I prefer to stand while I am thinking, so we set up an area across from Veronica's desk beside the whiteboard with a standing table for my papers and Bible. On the shelves below are multiple versions of the Bible, a concordance, Bible history books, Bible geography books, an Interlinear Hebrew/Greek/English Bible, and a Biblical archeology book. When we study the Word of God, we study it as completely as we can, with as many tools as we need to present the truth. We have been very good for each other in this respect. We have learned to listen to each other and to what God is putting into each of our hearts. The Scriptures are alive[7] for us, and it is where we find all of the answers we have needed to improve our lives. We know if we show women the evidence they need to see within the Scriptures, they too can use them to improve their lives. Veronica and I still help each other to improve by using Scripture.

We decided to analyze the scenarios as a whole and create one "Overcomer Training" package to suit all the scenarios. I had written the names of our clients and the scenarios in which they were working on the board when the landlady came through the door. I jumped into action to rub the names off before Dory saw them. Why did I not hear her come up the steps? *Note to self* – put a curtain rod over the white board with easy to close curtains in case this happens again. Our office is not large enough for a separate room for our discussions, so we must conduct our work in the same space we meet with our clients. We are going to have to do something about concealing our work from the general public who can walk in at anytime.

Our husbands have been quite handy since we opened Crown for Life. My husband has been the grunt worker, putting the desks together, carrying the heavy equipment around, moving furniture, and hanging all of our pictures, especially our mile long whiteboard. Veronica's husband has discovered we sometimes go the whole day without eating. He made us some super special microwavable lunches to freeze so we do not starve in our quest to help women. This has been a labour of love for all of us, other than this one thing – privacy is very important to us and we failed to see the threat this board could be to our clients. Any discussions are on hold until my husband Sam can hang a curtain rod above our white board.

I am breathing heavy when Dory steps up beside me. She eyes the board with a strange look. Dory said she has

---

[7] Hebrews 4:12

been married to Bert MacIntyre, our landlord, since the dinosaurs lived, but we think she is exaggerating a bit. They are a nice enough couple, but Dory has been up to our office every day since we moved in at unpredictable times, leaving me slightly uneasy. This is our first discussion I termed our "Revelation Rally" since we moved in. We had not predicted there would be complications. Previously, when we had them at my home office, we would close the door and not be disturbed, but, here at the office, it is not practical to lock the door. We were so caught up in our rally, we did not hear or see anyone coming up the steps. I was thinking that we could get away with adding a gate to the bottom of the stairs with some kind of noisemaker, and replace those curtains on the window next to the door with blinds, so we can see who has just come up the steps before they enter the office. Dory's "Stealth Bomber" way of getting into our office was on my mind as we said our farewells to Dory and returned to our work at hand. I kept all this information in my heart.

It was late Friday afternoon, so we locked the door, drew the curtains, and continued our discussion about Biblical boundaries. Every time we start using the board, Jesus gives us a revelation, so we put Him in charge of the board and called it "HeBoard." We pray before we start for His guidance about the plan He has for our clients. Veronica has a mind for words I cannot articulate, nor do I strive to. I give kooky names to our stuff so I do not have to remember those words. What she calls "board" I call "HeBoard", giving it a life of its own. God has made her and me so different yet the same, subsequently we are able to create and articulate descriptive tools for our clients.

When each of our clients left their first consultation, they were directed to journal everything they did, focusing on their disobedience to God. They are to return in one week to disclose what they have learned. More often than not, women will do the work, because by the time they seek our help they are at their wit's end with failing to do away with the behaviour God has required them to eliminate. We supplied them with personalized journals based on their specific individual need. On the first full page of each journal we hand wrote:

Week 1: Awareness Week

This week, you are becoming aware of the need for the White Picket Fence. With no fence to hold you back, you are free to roam into transgressions whether they work for you or not. Think this week about being surrounded by a White Picket Fence with our Lord as its foundation, and what a comfort it would be to have that fence surrounding you. Let us start first by going to the Word of God for the hope we will need to be successful.

God says in His Word, *No temptation has overtaken you except such as is common to man; but God is faithful, who will not allow you to be tempted beyond what you are able, but with the temptation will also make the way of escape, that you may be able to bear it* (1 Corinthians 10:1). Underline this verse in your Bible and read it at the beginning of each day so you can allow this hope to become truth in your mind. Highlight 'common to man' to know you are not alone, and the word 'make' that you understand there will always be a way out, ALWAYS. You can and will succeed, but only if you are aware of your transgressions. James 4:17 states *Therefore, to him who knows to do good and does not do it, to him it is sin.* If God has convicted you to make changes, He has made you aware of your transgression. From this day forward, your transgression is sin.

You are learning this week to be aware of your actions. Document everything that affects you. No secrets, because you cannot hide from God. No one will read this except you. Look up the Hope Verse and Fear Verse to write, word for word, in your journal. Choose which one will give you the most courage to continue.

Hope Verse: 1 Corinthians 10:13   Fear Verse: James 4:17

Document everything you do during each day that leads you to your sin below your chosen verse. Rewrite your chosen verse at the beginning of each day. Trust Him this week for hope, and trust us this week to help you become aware.

Signed, Leola and Veronica

With that written in their book, we scheduled appointments for them in the following week, beginning Tuesday. The six-week plan God has given us from the Scriptures will help them change their life forever, should they submit to God and to the plan. What we expect will happen to each of them during this first week was correctly predicted. I have been through this before, and Veronica is going through it now. History is telling me that if they do their work, they will get the same result. We instructed each of the women to be patient with themselves during this process. They have taken years to develop these habits, and it will take more than six weeks to be delivered from them, but if they truly long for freedom, they shall have it under the tutelage of our Lord Jesus Christ.

3
WHAT SPARKS A FIRE

I could not get "HeBoard" off my mind until we did something about it. Dory told us Friday that she would not be home on Sunday because of a church function she and Bert were to attend, so we chose to make the changes to the office Sunday after church. Before I went home Friday night, I went to the store to purchase a wooden curtain rod and some curtains to hang over "HeBoard". While Sam and I worked on "HeBoard's" curtain, Andrew and Veronica worked on removing the curtains and installing a blind on the stair window. Then us women admired the new curtains with a fresh cup of coffee, while the men installed the gate at the bottom of the steps. After searching the store on Saturday with Sam, we came up with an idea to run fishing line along the step to a bell located inside the office, 'dinging' when the gate is opened and alerting us to a guest. Sam opened the gate and sure enough the bell rang, *ding*. Not too loud, but loud enough for us to hear and take the required action to assure our clients' privacy at all times. I looked around the office before locking the door, and my "intuitive antenna" went up about something I could not quite put my finger on. I kept this odd feeling in my heart for future reference.

With the new gate installed, Marg, the dog from across the street, also could not come up the steps without her master, or at least that is what I thought. Bright and early Monday morning, I opened the gate and listened for the sound of the bell. Barely, but I heard the ding. The low sound outside was needed because we didn't want Dory to know we had a way of un-stealthing her bombings. I got the coffee going, opened my Bible, and stared out at the early birds getting their feed. I opened the curtains on "HeBoard", and did the Monday morning super clean. I am pretty particular about this board. I cannot write on it unless it is perfectly white with no streaks or colour remnants from our last rally. I was reminded about how close we had come, and just had to practice how fast I could close the curtains if I heard someone coming up the stairs. I am also particular about planning. Ready, set, ding. Curtain closed, one second, curtain closed, two seconds. Not enough information for my peculiar mind. I went down the stairs and left the door open to see how long it would take for someone to run up the stairs. Ready, set, ding – bang, bang, bang, bang, bang. Four seconds. I was busy inspecting my watch when I saw Marg run past me into the office. What? Did I leave the gate open? A quick look tells me I didn't. Then how is it Marg is in this office, wagging her tail like she has not seen me for a year? I went into the office to ask her how she got in when I heard the ding. I watched the window to see who it was, as if I had no idea. I counted to five seconds before Henry came through the door with a smile on his face.

"I see you put a gate up. Are you trying to keep Marg out or Dory?" he asked with that smile still planted on his face.

I returned his smile with my sheepish smile, "I thought Marg might be a bonus to having the gate. How did she get through it?"

"She didn't go through, she went over. She used to jump six-foot fences, so your two-foot gate is a plaything for her. The fishing line to the bell is a good idea. You should have plenty of time to prepare for Dory," Smarty-pants said. I forgot that Henry had already told us Marg was a retired police dog, so his description of how Marg got in should not have surprised me at all. Henry walked to the coffee pot while he was talking to pour himself a coffee, sat in Veronica's guest chair, and put his feet up on her desk. I am having a hard time believing this man is in his sixties. He is about six-foot-two, with the physique of a thirty-five-year-old, not a sixty-something retired Army Sergeant who watches *The Red Green Show* night and day.

We talked about nothing in particular until he was done his coffee, then he left with Marg in tow. I was pondering if Henry knew Jesus while watching him from my window, when I heard the ding. Counting to seven, I saw Veronica's head in the window. I am now convinced I can close the curtains on "HeBoard" long before anyone can get up those steps. "Good Morning," I said.

"Back at ya. Did the gate ding?" she queried.

"Yes, it did." I said with a huge smile. "I timed everything. We are good." Unfortunately for Veronica, she knew exactly what I did to accomplish that task. This was not her first rodeo with me. She shook her head, and I smiled to confirm her notions.

We got right to work getting ready for our first client to come tomorrow for week two of our plan. Week two is not as easy as week one. I opened the curtains again on "HeBoard" so we could have a "Revelation Rally" to find further information in the Scriptures about setting personal Biblical boundaries. Our rally was productive in preparing ourselves for our first of four clients on this subject to arrive tomorrow. We decided to lock up early when we heard the ding. One. Two. Three. Four. Five. Six. Dory. Seven. In the door, "Hi, Dory. How are you today?" Veronica said.

"I'm okay. Why did you put a gate at the bottom of the stairs? For Margret Thatcher? Marg used to jump six-foot fences, so your gate will not be a problem for her. She is a retired police dog, you know. Henry adopted her after his wife died. He was lonely. He used to drink a lot without his wife, then he got Marg and he stopped drinking to take care of her. He would die without her," Dory said, then immediately put her head down, whispered something we could not hear, but I did hear the word journal. My "intuitive antenna" went right up.

"Yes, I found out this morning. She came up to visit me." I said nicely, hoping she would not assume the gate was for her, but she was busy chatting to herself.

Finally, when she looked up, she said, "I see you are all packed to leave, so I will let you go. I cleaned on Saturday. You women are pretty clean, so it took hardly any time to get done. The downstairs office, on the other hand, is a huge mess by Saturday, and it takes most of my time to clean. Those people do not know what clean is. I do not think their parents taught them anything of use. Did you know we have gay neighbours? They own the house next door. That is why the house is blue and has lots of flowers. One of them likes to garden and the other one likes light colours." As we headed to the door, she pointed out the window, "There they are now. Look at the shirt Jaime has on. It is so tight. Rats, I did it again." She looked intently at me with wide eyes.

We continued out the door and down the steps to the gate. I opened the gate, praying Dory would not hear the ding inside the office. Veronica and I walked to our cars while Dory headed to her house. I waved at the neighbours and closed my car door. I waited for Veronica to back out before I did. Dory looked back at me with a dejected look on her face. Dory has said some very peculiar things today outside of her typical gossip. My "intuitive antenna" seems to go up every time Dory is around.

The next morning, I played the counting game. It still took me four seconds at a full gallop, a full two seconds more than it takes to close the curtains on "HeBoard". I nodded my head with satisfaction while I unlocked the door and walked to the coffee pot. A few minutes later, with coffee in hand, I sat at my desk thinking about what has happened over the last week. I am so blessed by God to sit in this seat, watching the early birds; it brings me to tears. "Stop that, girl. You will ruin your makeup," I spoke to myself sternly.

Ding. I ignore it because I know Veronica is making her way up. She texted me to tell me she is coming early so we can discuss, again, how we will proceed and make changes, if needed, prior to Gladys Pender's arrival. Her appointment is at 9:00a.m., and it is now 7:30a.m. Veronica is a bit of a worrywart about what we produce because she cares so deeply about our clients. She will lose sleep over what we have created, worried about its effect on them. I wonder if this is what happened last night? One good look at her tells me the answer to that question. She looks like she spent the whole night on the computer, checking our work.

"Oh, my. Did you not sleep last night?"

"No, but I am so stoked about meeting Gladys today. I think what we have done is going to work for her." She said with her big, white smile as she walked into the bathroom to apply her makeup.

When she came out of the bathroom, I said, "Wowsa! How do you transform your image from dead tired to supermodel in so little time?"

"I pay big bucks to create this miracle," she said as she headed for the coffee pot.

We sat down at our respective desks, and I listened as Veronica regaled me with why she is so convinced what we have will work for Gladys and the other clients. Her main reason is because she spent the night trying to refute it. She went through last week's assignment, along with the women, because she wants to work on how many times she says something negative. She was absolutely shocked by how many times in one day she uttered negative words. We decided, as a team, only one of us would go through a new process while the other observed. Observing and documenting the changes is just as important as doing it. Will it work for the bystander too? In other words, will their respective families notice the change as well? Veronica became aware of her sin. First goal accomplished.

Ding. I looked at my watch. It is nine o'clock already? I looked at the window to see a pink hat with lilac ribbon encircling the crown of the hat. The brim was long enough to keep the sun out of her eyes. Gladys is dressed as if she was born into a family of millionaires. Each time we have seen her, she was wearing skirt suits we guessed were designer, costing more than our rent. She opened the door and walked in already, saying, "Ladies, I am so disappointed in myself." She had a frown so deep we thought she would begin to cry, but she just sat down in my guest chair in front of the window and stared at the birds coming back to feed.

Gladys Pender came to Crown for Life two weeks ago, after reading our ad in *The Shepherd's Guide*. She told us of her struggle with an issue she thought was hidden from everyone else. She did everything she could to explain her problem without crying. After one hour of beating around the bush, she finally confessed she is a spend thrift, and God has convicted her to deal with it. She told us everyday she would vow not to spend and every day she spent just a little more than the day before. She had no idea how much she was spending until she had to write down everything she was doing this past week. This, she finally divulges after multiple attempts, is why she is so disappointed. Gladys has trouble getting right to the point because it is too shocking for her. She talks in circles until she confuses everyone, including herself. Unfortunately for her, we are clear as to what her problem is, so we ask questions until it is clear to her. The goal of week one is to recognize our sin, not to cover it up.

When we gave her the journal, we told her not to change a thing, but to document what she buys and how much it costs. She described her week for us: "On Wednesday, I woke up with my same conviction not to spend, but according to my journal I spent $79.00. I went to bed dejected and renewed my vow. I woke up Thursday again with my daily vow, but according to my journal, I spent $84.15. By now, I am over the top angry about my lack of will power to curtail my spending, even though I know you told me not to change. Friday was the same, as well as Saturday and Sunday. Monday, I stayed home in disappointment. Everything I see I want to buy because I am not supposed to buy. I feel I need to tell you this. My husband and I are wealthy, so my small amount of spending is not a drain on our supply, but God, in His ultimate wisdom, has convicted me to get control. I think He has a plan for my money rather than to make all the store owners in Essex County wealthy." We prayed with Gladys as she left with her week two plan. Veronica and I also prayed for her once she was gone.

Wednesday came as we sat in the office waiting for Dee Zurtaker to arrive for her appointment. She had heard about us at her church and decided to call us. We sent some flyers to the churches in Essex County, who promised they would post them on their bulletin boards. She has been struggling with something no one else understands. She has been without support from the beginning, but Jesus still wants her to obey. Veronica and I know just as well as anyone else, when God convicts, He means it, and He will not let up until we comply. We believed Dee, and heard her out on her first visit. She has an idol, God told her, and it is desserts. She thinks about sweets all the time to distraction, she has discovered. We know her dilemma.

Ding. I have become accustomed to counting and watching the window to find out how long it takes each individual to ascend the steps until I see their beautiful face in the window. Dee has a hairstyle from the sixties, and she wears a pair of reading glasses as a necklace. Looking at her slim figure, we would never have guessed she was struggling with eating too many sweets, but we know skinny doesn't always equate to healthy. She tells us her story: "This week has been a great eye-opener for me. I was not aware of how many times per day I stopped what I am doing to eat something sweet. If I do not have sweets in the house, I will go right to the store to buy some. I was ignorant of my behaviour until God brought it to my attention through this journal. I had no idea how much this need for a sweet has occupied my thoughts and invaded my life. Sunday, during church, all I could think about was the desserts waiting in the gym for the Strawberry Social. God is correct in telling me that they have become my idol. I heard not one word of the sermon because my mind was preoccupied with the ice cream and cake. When Jesus asked me if I had any idols before Him, I honestly said 'no', but he has enlightened me, and so has this journal. I am dedicated to eliminating this idol. I love Jesus and do not want to have any other idols before Him." We discussed Dee's week further and heard great conviction in her voice and stance. We know she will be successful at eliminating this idol from her life. We discussed week two with her, prayed, and sent her on her way to get started. Veronica and I prayed for her after she left as well.

Thursday brought us to the day Mary Touchier was to visit with her journal. She is a very gregarious woman and filled with love for people. She has been told that her ungoverned touching of people is making them feel invaded. She does it out of love and is mortified that they feel invaded. She cannot believe people feel that way about being loved. The last time she was told about her invasion, she felt a great conviction from God to make changes. She cried for days because she could not show the love she so dearly wants to lavish on them. God has convicted her to learn about love in all forms. She has tried to stop touching, but it has become a habit for her. Mary tells us her story: "I have been so close to my mother and father in a physical way and felt so loved. I just wanted to give that same loving feeling to others. I documented everything I have done this week. I hugged a child, touched a mommy belly, hugged an elderly man, and touched a newborn. I love touching people. I feel loved at the end of the day when I touch people and they touch me. I know they love it too, but God has convicted me to stop touching people. Why am I not allowed to show love to people? But I will do it; just as Peter threw his net out at the

Word of Jesus,[8] I will stop touching people at the Word of Jesus." She is confused about why God has convicted her to change, but she loves God and is willing to make the changes for Him. Experience tells us that God will reveal why He is requiring this of her. We sent her off with prayer and her week two assignments. We allowed her to hug us good-bye. We prayed again for her after she left.

    We are invigorated and exhausted by Friday, as we drink our morning coffee, awaiting the ding. Nicole Teen, our fourth client, is young but a mature Christian. She has a habit she has tried to kick for a couple of years but cannot seem to do it. She is a smoker and loves the smell of cigarette smoke, which is a major reason she has not been able to quit. The smell draws her back every single time. God has convicted her to quit, but, after months of failed attempts, she came to us for help. I know exactly where she is coming from, as an ex-smoker myself. Her week has helped her to learn a few things about documenting. She doesn't journal about anything, not even about what she learns reading the Bible. We asked her to journal about when she smokes and how much she spends. She tells us how it went: "I was annoyed to do this. I hate writing. I would rather do this on the computer, but I can't carry my computer with me everywhere I go. I knew I wouldn't remember everything, so I wrote as you instructed. Carrying this book around with me was a pain, but I got used to it, and began grabbing it out of habit every time I grabbed my cigarettes. I am intrigued about how much information I was able to glean about myself during this time. Writing my life down taught me more than how much I smoke but how much I actually spend on it too. I never counted the financial cost of smoking before because I just bought what I needed. Do you know if I quit smoking and saved the money instead I would have a good down payment for a starter home in one year?" Nicole is getting the picture. I quit when the cigarettes got to $5.00 a pack, and I

---

[8] Luke 5:5 NKJV

cannot imagine how much money people are spending today for them. The health risks are staggering as well. We pray with her and she collects her week two assignments and leaves. I watched her in the window as she lit a cigarette, thinking, with a smile, she will be free of that nasty habit soon. Veronica and I prayed for her and rested. It has been a long week.

We later discussed what Veronica wrote in all the journals. As we adventure into this new business, we are finding what our weaknesses and our strengths are. We are falling into position based on our gifts, and it is working well for our clients. We discovered with the writing of week one's journal notes, Veronica is obviously the better one to do the writing; my handwriting resembles a doctor's. She read week two's note for me:

Week 2 - Spark Week

You are now aware of the need for the "White Picket Fence", based on what you have learned from week one's journaling. What are the sparks[9] that will burn down your fence? You need to discover what is behind your failure to succeed, because once you raise a fence you <u>do not</u> want to burn it down out of ignorance. Knowledge is power.

There are two references to fire in the Bible with regards to God. The first is His judgment against those who ignore His commandments (John 15:6), and the second is His presence (Acts 2:3). God is ever present in your life, therefore Acts 2:3 will be your Hope Verse this week, and Isaiah 50:11 will be your Fear Verse. Look them both up in your Bible and heed them this week. Write whichever one you need to use at the top of your journal each day this week before you start journaling.

You are learning this week what sparks a fire in you to sin. Continue journaling this week. Write the Hope Verse:

---

[9] Spark is what causes us to do what we don't want to do. A trigger.

Acts 2:3 or the Fear Verse: Isaiah 50:11 in your journal at the beginning of each day. Make a chart with three columns, the same as the chart shown below. In column one, you will document what you did. You can use as few or as many words as you need for a full understanding. In column two, you will document whom you were with and what was happening when you did what you did. In column three, you will document your feelings when you did what you did. Your feelings are very important to discover because they can be modified, given the correct information about them. Remember, knowledge is power.

What did I do?	Who was I with and what was happening?	What was I feeling?

Be patient with yourself. You did not get to this point in your life overnight, and you will not change overnight either, but you can enlighten yourself enough to make sure you are successful at eliminating your sin.

May the Lord and the process be with you.

Signed, Leola and Veronica

I asked, "Veronica, how are you doing?" She has been showing each lady her own personal journal to help them complete theirs. This has been rough on her emotionally because she is not used to asking for help; she is more accustomed to giving it. She is also not accustomed to making her own struggles public knowledge, but she knows that to be able to help women get through all of their hurt, she has to wear hers on her sleeve. I have been working on my struggles and hurt for as long as I have been walking with Jesus, so I know exactly what she is going through.

"This has been a tough week. My heart not only hurts because of what I have learned about myself, but for them too. This process is not easy, but I know it is so important for us to go through. I know you have done all this before; how did you get through it?" She volleyed back at me. She has a good way of deflecting before she cries.

"I went through every bit of pain you are going through. I cried and yelled at God to take it away. I had no idea when I was going through it I would be studying the Scriptures for other women so they could go through it with less agony than I did. If I would have known I may not have done so much kicking and screaming." I laughed, knowing that probably would not be true. "I was a sucky baby and handled it much worse than you. You are much stronger than I was. My childish behaviour sometimes even disgusted me." I stared out the window to thank Jesus for getting me through all the pain in one piece. I looked back at Veronica and she was silently crying. I got up and held her until she stopped. I cannot take the pain from her, but I can love her through it just as Jesus loved me. We talked for hours after that.

4
ALLOWING INTERVENTION

After our long discussion, Veronica and I agreed to talk to each other about the emotional havoc helping women develop Biblical Life Skills would have on us personally. We needed to be honest about it and pray for each other daily. Last week was an emotional week for me too, although not to the extent that it was for Veronica or our clients. I spent the weekend with my husband, recovering from the exhaustion my emotions can have on me. Monday came much too quickly for me. As I sat in my window seat watching the birds, I was reminded about the weekend and how comforting my husband had been. I prayed this weekend for each of our clients and Veronica. I know exactly what each one of them is feeling. It can be frustrating and lonely learning how to undo what we have done to upend our life. It is still hard to look back on my own learning. I fully understand today the agony I endured to become the "me" that I am. My heart breaks for these women, all women, who must go through this to make sure they will become the women God has created them to be. I know this will be the best thing to happen to them. I want that for each woman who requests my help. Together, we are going to learn to live a stronger, more determined life.

Neither Veronica nor I were prepared for the emotional strain this past week would have on us. We must have emotional downtime blocked out in our weekly schedule. Our daily plan has never included time to unwind, but it will now. It is heart-breaking to watch our clients discover their own weaknesses and their helplessness up until this point. What they have done to their lives by making bad decisions has resulted in who they are today. I was not prepared for my own agony due to my foolishness either. I spent my whole life making foolish decisions that would hurt me in the end. The consequences of those bad decisions came back to haunt me for years. I am still paying the price for some of them today, physically and emotionally. I never took into consideration that the decisions I was making then would have consequences years down the road. Learning to make wise decisions modified some consequences, but some had to remain as a reminder of my foolishness.

When God called me, He began training me to make decisions based on His Word rather than the world. I did not know what the difference was until I started reading the Bible. I thought I was a good person who had decent morals, but it turned out my morals had miles to go to become righteous, and my boundaries did not keep me safe. I have walked the same walk Veronica and all these other women are following now. I remember how hard every day was, doing what God had required of me.

The rain outside was reflected in my heart, so I turned to the One who has saved me with His Word before and who will comfort me again. I thank Him for who He has made me into today because I am very happy with the new me. I suffered, but I have overcome. I smile, knowing all the women we help will overcome as well, should they persevere. I open my Bible to Isaiah 50:7: *For the Lord God will help Me; therefore I will not be disgraced; therefore I will set my face like a flint and I know that I will not be ashamed.* I set my face like a flint to do everything I can to help every woman who comes to

Crown for Life for our help. My emotions will not stop me from being who these women need me to continue to be. Jesus is my Redeemer, and He will be theirs as well. Ding.

Strengthened by God, I looked toward the kitchen window to see who was walking up the steps. I knew it was not Veronica because she would be here at noon. It was not someone I recognized through the window, but I was certain I would know her in one second. The door opened and she stepped inside the office. "I have wanted to see this office for a couple of weeks," she said as she continued to walk toward me with her hand out in front of her. I stood to shake her hand. "My name is Tabitha. This place is fantastic. Love what you did with this wall." She pointed at "HeBoard's" curtains. I didn't feel I needed to say anything yet. "We have the office downstairs. Fabio, Willie, and I were wondering who you are and what you do. We have seen women coming and going, assuming this is some feminist project," she smiled.

My smile widened, knowing we had been wondering the same thing about them. Since we enter through the rear of the building and they enter through the front, we have not seen them, just as they have not seen us. One day we would hear activity in their office, and the next, quiet. We could not even guess what kind of work they did, so we had not tried. "My name is Leola, and my partner is Veronica. We have named our business Crown for Life. We are serving Jesus Christ by helping women do what God has required of them. We supply them a plan to work with until they can discern the plan God has for them from His Word." I pointed to our Mission Statement on the wall. "What are you peeps doing down there?"

She laughed, "I am an Occasion Organizer who specializes in non-profit events, and I will do weddings if I have to. Fabio is a personal trainer who makes house calls. Willie is a freelance writer. I am not sure if she specializes in any kind of writing. She has been published in many different types of newspapers, as well as online. She loves researching. They are both downstairs if you want to meet them." I nodded my head, and she turned on her stiletto heels toward the door.

We headed downstairs, talking about our additions to the office. Tabitha also made a comment about the gate keeping Dory out. I can tell Dory is not highly liked in this neighbourhood. We have been praying for her every day, as well as the rest of our neighbours. We don't really know any of them well, but that will not stop us from praying for them. Tabitha and I walked through the side door into their office. I could not believe what I was looking at! According to Tabitha, they bought the furniture from a bankrupt coffee shop in the City of Windsor, close to our office. I was flabbergasted at the wonderfully stimulating atmosphere. She took me on a very exciting tour and introduced me to both of her officemates. They work on bar-height, shiny, metal-top tables with red trim. How fascinating. There is a foot bar around the center post at the bottom, just like in the old soda shops from the 1960s. I was in love. The coffee machine was also super cool. It made every kind of coffee; I dare not try to even remember the names of them all. They offered but I declined, for now. "This office is fantastic. I love everything you have done. The colours, the furniture, and the walls," I said, continuing to look around. They added a wonderful touch by hanging pictures of country cafes located in Paris and Venice. Ooh la la!

"Thank you." Tabitha said, with pride in her voice.

"We might be working in a fun office," Willie said, "but we still have to find someplace to pitch our skills. Tabitha can occasionally bring her clients here, but I cannot bring anyone here. My potential clients are old and stuffy, born in the sixties and seventies. If they saw where I did my writing, they would question the seriousness of my work."

My brain cogs were cogging as I said, "I have an idea to help you, but I need to talk with Veronica first." At that, we parted ways, and I went upstairs to read the Bible and pray about the potentially wonderful idea that I had, to see if it was from God. I think Veronica will like it, but I needed to show her the office before she would approve.

I went upstairs to read and pray. Dory worked her way up the steps after I was warned by the ding. She looks gloomy today. She strolled to the coffee pot to pour herself a coffee before she walked to my guest chair. As she sat down, I asked, "Why are you gloomy today?" Does gloomy weather make for a gloomy Dory?

Dory looked at me with pain in her eyes. "You know I am not well liked in this neighbourhood. When I walk up to people talking, they stop talking. People make mean comments to me when they talk to me, too."

"I am so sorry, Dory," I said, not meaning to be a poet. "How long have you been feeling on the outs with the neighbours?"

"I noticed it about a month ago when Brandon and Jaime stopped greeting me, and now they do not talk to me at all. Henry will not talk to me either, but he at least lets Marg come to see me. She is such a lovely dog. Those people downstairs actually asked me if I was visiting them to snoop when I just came to see if the toilet was working just a few minutes ago. Bert fixed it on the weekend because it was running all the time." Huge breath. "Henry told me you put the gate up to keep me out. Is that true?" she sniffed.

I guess Henry was talking to her long enough to tease her. "Does it keep you out?" I asked.

"Of course not. It isn't even locked." Dory said through her tears.

I handed her a tissue before I spoke. "Dory, the truth is that we put the gate up as a result of your unnoticed visits, but not to stop you. We had our clients' confidentiality in mind when we installed the gate. It is a warning to us of anyone coming up, not just you." Ding. Both of us looked at the bell. "Someone has just come through the gate. I now know what I need to do if I am writing on the board or already have a client sitting here. Do you understand? Remember when you came up and we were writing on the board – that, my lovely, was not a good situation. We were concentrating on what we were doing, and not on who might be able to come in to see confidential information. The gate was not about you personally." I stared at her to see if she understood what I was telling her. I really want her to know it was not her fault; it was our fault.

"Hi, Veronica. You have a very good warning system with that gate and the bell," Dory said, revealing to me she fully understood. "Let me help you with those bags." She got up to take some bags from Veronica. "Mmmm, that smells lovely."

"Yes, it does, and I had to drive all the way over here with this food without touching it. Andrew, my husband, made us some food to freeze so we don't miss lunch," Veronica said while she began unloading the food to store in the refrigerator and freezer. I love the food Andrew makes for us. My mouth was watering already in anticipation for lunch.

Dory put the food down on the counter and looked at me with a smile. She came back over to sit in front of me with a look I can only describe as guilt. I assumed the look was from asking the question about the gate. She chitchatted with us for a few more minutes and excused herself so we could eat one of those lunches. My "intuitive antenna" went up, despite her confession of neighbourhood drama. There was definitely something else going on with Dory I could not figure out. I would have to talk to Veronica later so we could pray for her and about her. God gave Daniel, Hananiah, Mishael, and Azariah the knowledge of Nebuchadnezzar's dream in Daniel Chapter 2 when they asked for it, and I am well aware that God can enlighten us about what is bothering Dory. I feel like she wants to tell me something else, but I cannot guess about what it might be.

While we ate our delicious lunches, we talked about the weekend and how we had both felt exhausted from the emotional week before. I told her we need to make a habit of including time in our schedule for "Emotional Down Time", which I had already renamed "Emodoe Time". We cannot get overloaded with our own emotions. We will become ineffective to those who need us. This could include alone time or together time, talking about what is affecting our peace. The peace of God must remain in this office or women will come in and feel something is amiss right away. When they feel angst in our office, they will not be able to deal with their own emotions correctly. We need them to feel peace with the freedom to say what they need to say. They need to know what they say will not be held against them at any time. As long as we keep the peace Jesus gave us[10] in this office, we will be able to assure our clients of their own coming peace.

After lunch, we opened "HeBoard" and began talking about what we expected to happen this week. We anticipated that the women who are following along would make some new discoveries about what makes them do what they do not want to do. We all have something to trigger us to sin, and we are learning how to recognize the spark that can set our whole life on fire. When that spark happens, we need to recognize the consequences of reacting in our typical way. We will never be able to change our way if we do not see what sparks are flying before we do the thing that leads us to sin. We discussed Veronica's week discovering her sparks. She had a wonderful chart created, counting how many times she spoke negatively to others.

"I am sensitive now about what I say," Veronica said. "Every time I say something the least bit negative, God convicts me. I don't know how to stop it yet, but God has made me aware of it." She smiled when she spoke, but I know how hard this is for her because she does not like people to know she lacks control. She likes people to think she is in control at all times. When it is apparent she is not in control, she loses control of her emotions, she is learning. God is showing her, through helping women, she is not alone in her struggles.

---

[10] John 14:27

One of the things God is working with me on is allowing God to do His works in His way. I have memorized Psalm 131,[11] which beckons me to not ..._concern myself with great matters, Nor with things too profound for me._ If I want my soul to be calm and quiet, I need to allow God's plan for each person to work itself out. God's plan is of great matter to everyone, and it is absolutely too profound for me. This means I need to allow God to train His women in His time, not mine. If I get a conviction to keep my thoughts to myself, I do, because His thoughts are much greater than mine,[12] and He knows His thoughts[13] for each person. Veronica and our clients are not the only ones learning. I spend plenty of my time learning from the Lord every day.

Tuesday we started our third visit with these particular clients. We have been talking about what to expect and how each woman may react to last week's work, based on how they reacted to the first week's tasks. They all learned something significant and the great idea about the office downstairs has fallen right into place for next week. Ding.

Gladys walked into the office with less pomp this week. "God has been speaking to me this week," she said with great joy. I smiled at her. Her clothing looks much more sedate and much less expensive.

"Good Morning, Gladys." I said with a loving smile. "We are very excited about God speaking to you. We love it when God speaks to us and we are more than happy He is speaking to you. What has God been telling you this week?" I asked with the same smile she saw when she came in. I am happy to see her and happy to know her.

"Well, He started talking to me the day I started documenting my spending by making my stomach go bonkers every time I bought something. I did not know it was Him until this past week, when He did the same thing to

---

[11] Psalm 131:1
[12] Isaiah 55:8-9
[13] Jeremiah 29:11

me at the mall. I was intent on buying this wonderful purple suit when my stomach started getting queasy. I do not like it when my stomach is upset and He knows it. Anyway, I walked over to the suit I wanted to buy and it got worse, much worse, if you know what I mean?" We nodded, and she continued. "I had to leave, but as soon as I sat in my car the queasiness went away, so I headed back into the store. Sure enough, as soon as I stood in front of that suit again it came right back. I am convinced it was God because I walked away from the suit, went to my car, and it went away for the second time. I got this feeling of peace about leaving it behind though, so I left the store and didn't look back. I had no idea that God did stuff like that."

"I think God will do what He needs to do to cause us to be obedient. He has told you to be wise with your money. He apparently did not think buying the suit was a wise thing to do, I would suspect, based on your little experience," I laughed.

She showed us her chart. She is starting to see God all over this. Gladys is a very particular woman and very articulate at record keeping. She spends a lot of time pondering her work to figure out why she does what she does. She is a model client. We do not always get clients who will do the work like Gladys has. Sometimes our clients will not do the rest of the work because it hurts too much, but Gladys is not one of them.

"Based on my chart, I can tell you when I am bored, I spend money. I did not know that until this week. I was unaware that I was bored. Maybe I am just bored all the time because I am not as active as I used to be. I wish I did more, but I do not know what to do. Can you pray for God to show me what to do? I will listen. I am listening," she said, holding back tears. We said we would be honored to pray for her, and we talked about week three's assignment. We prayed with her about the knowledge she had already gained and the new knowledge she would gain. We asked her if we could meet next Thursday afternoon rather than Tuesday morning. She agreed, and off she went.

Wednesday came, and so did Dee with her revelations from God. She walked up with her chart in hand and a bounce in her step. She has been tracking her need to eat desserts. She calls herself a tweet-a-holic with the "Tweety Bird" accent. She is such a cutie pie. Her recollection of the week is scattered, but she does know she eats too many 'tweets.' She is going to find out this week if she can get some control. Unfortunately, Dee discovered this past week she eats without any cause. As much as she tried to figure out what was causing her to eat them, she was unsuccessful. She has chalked it up to habit and that she loves them, but not more than Jesus. She counted how many times she eats sweets in one day and the minimum was five. We prayed with her to get back to her first love, Jesus. We asked her to come next Thursday afternoon and sent her off with week three tasks. "I am going to conquer this," she said on her way out, with a smile.

Thursday turned out to be almost the same experience as Tuesday and Wednesday. Mary touches people too much and she learned in her first week exactly how much she touches people without being aware of it. She is a habitual toucher and God has demanded she stop. He has performed miraculous things in Mary's life this week too. Mary had a dream last Friday night she knew was from God. As she sat down in Veronica's guest chair, she told us about it.

"In my dream, God made me stand in the middle of my backyard by myself. I could not see His face, but I know it was Him. There was such peace in my mind standing alone, waiting for Him to touch me. I knew He was going to touch me because He told me He would, and I should feel loved by His touch alone." She put her hand on her heart and said, "He touched me right here." A tear ran down her cheek as she pointed to her heart.

God, through this dream, helped her to understand she wants to touch people because she does not feel loved. People touching her makes her feel loved, but she is to wait for the touch of God. He is the only one who can love her completely. She has never felt this loved before. She did not understand last week, but this week God has been so gracious as to explain it to her. Previously, she was angry with God for taking this from her, but now she understands. She was putting too much pressure on other people for love. Her heart is right with Jesus. We prayed with her about her tasks for next week, and I gave her some helpful books to read from our library regarding love. We asked her to meet us Thursday at one o'clock in the afternoon instead of morning. She agreed and left us uplifted. We can see Jesus working miracles with Mary.

We had two surprises on Friday. Our first was the excitement Nicole brought. She came first thing in the morning because she was super stoked to come and show us her chart. She reminded us that she has not at all been happy with handwriting notes but would rather use the computer or her phone, typing. "Typing is faster and more efficient," she had said. She discovered something peculiar about writing with a pen. She smokes less. Her chart indicated she was a chain smoker while she was on the computer and did not smoke at all while she was writing. She hasn't had a cigarette in two weeks before she goes to sleep, because she made a habit of writing just before bed. Another thing she has been doing more while writing is talking to God, and He has been talking to her. She came to the conclusion that she smokes to have something to do with her hands. She, it turns out, is a fidgeter. This is a great revelation for her because she has never been able to figure out why she smokes, outside of loving the smell. She just does it and has not been able to quit. She thinks it might very well be possible now. I have not seen her smile so much. We prayed with her and sent her out to do the week three assignment with an agreed upon Thursday afternoon meeting. She was more excited to get the work this week and she did not even light a cigarette when she walked out the door. I am very pleased for her.

Veronica and I heard the ding as we watched Nicole

leave. We heard talking; we could not understand what was being said, but we saw Dory through the window. We have not seen Dory since Monday. She stood by the door as if she wanted to say something, but she did not talk; she just looked at us. I am not sure if she is going to smile or cry; she looks awful. She stood looking at us for what seemed like an hour, except it was only a few minutes. I have never been good at tracking time when I am uncomfortable.

"I have something to tell you. I have been watching women come out of this office all week." Both Veronica and I are looking at her with perplexed looks on our face. "When you first opened this office, I was skeptical about what you were doing up here. I honestly thought you planned to take advantage of women. I had convinced myself of your deception. Searching through your drawers became God's work to me, except what I really found was God's work in those drawers. I never looked at your client's papers. I might be a gossiper, but I know what confidentiality means. It was not my intention to invade their privacy, just expose your deception." She had just stunned us. She looked at both of us to see us staring at her with our mouths wide open. She started laughing at the picture.

"I know! Is it not the craziest thing?" She was still laughing, and when she stopped she continued, "I saw what you were doing with these ladies. I had discovered you were working hard to help these women, but I could not face it. I started working your plan just to prove it wrong. I bought myself a book and started writing. I thought for sure you had caught me a couple of times because you looked at me like you knew exactly what I was doing, Leola. Each time I came up here to talk to you, God convicted me to tell you, but I was scared to admit what I did. I kept doing what you had told these women to do, and it did something for me. I have discovered I gossip because I am afraid people will not like me, so I beat them to it by disliking them first. Every time I feel intimidated by someone, I gossip about them. I am so sad to say, I apparently do not like too many people, but honestly, I do. God laid such a conviction on me to tell you, I have not slept since Monday. That is four nights and I am sure I would not be able to sleep tonight either if I had not given in to God." She took a deep breath and said, "I am so sorry I deceived you, and I brought money to pay you for everything I have done so far. I am also here to beg you to take me on as a client. I talked to that woman on the stairs and she looked so happy and content. I want that."

Dory had sat in her usual seat across from me. I think she likes looking outside too when she thinks. I looked at her with compassion because, as she was telling us this story, God gave me such a love for her. I felt like my heart was going to explode with compassion for her.

"Did you bring your book with you?" I asked with a smile.

She jostled around in her purse for a few seconds and pulled out a book that was exactly the same as the ones we were using. "I do not go anywhere without it because I do not go anywhere without my mouth. The chart I made really helped me to understand why I gossip." She opened her book to the page she had drawn her chart on. Dory pointed to the third column. "Look at these words: intimidated, useless, scared, insecure. I am a mess, but God has been speaking to me this week. He had confidence in me when I had no confidence in myself. God loves me, and I should share that love."

We took Dory on as a client and told her to come back next Thursday afternoon after she works out week three's tasks. We sent each woman off, including Dory now, with a new handwritten note in their books that said:

Week 3 - Intervention Week

You have now become aware, not only of how much this transgression has affected you every day, but also what sparks a fire under you to do it. We cannot do anything about this behaviour if we never attempt to stop it. We are going to have a two-fold intervention this week. First, you are going to attempt to intervene on your own behalf, then, second, you will allow Jesus to intervene on your behalf as well. Isaiah 43:19 says *Behold, I will do a new thing, Now it shall spring forth; Shall you not know it? I will even make a road in the wilderness And rivers in the desert.* Just for you.

You are learning this week to allow intervention into the behaviours that lead you into sin. Continue journaling this week with the Hope Verse: Isaiah 43:19, or the Fear Verse: Proverbs 25:28, to begin your day. Make a chart with three columns the same as the chart shown below. In column one, you will write your attempts at change. Do not think about them, just write them and try not to do the same thing the next day. If you do, document it. In column two, document whether it worked with Y or N. In column three, document how hard it was for you to make that attempt at change with 1 being easy and 10 being hard. You will continue to journal this week as well. Again, I will remind you, knowledge is power.

Attempts at change	Did it work?	Easy 1-10 Hard

Pay close attention for the intervention of Jesus this week and begin reading your Bible every day. An intervention from Jesus can look like anything that makes you feel uncomfortable, such as the sweats, stomach problems, the jitters, an instant guilty feeling, or something like that to make you uncomfortable. It will be personal, and it will be effective. It might take some time for you to discern that it is Jesus, but allow Him to guide you through it.

You have two additional assignments for next week. Please bring a frontal picture of yourself smiling, no smaller than 3" x 3". You will also need to know what is on the other side of this transgression. Sit with Jesus in a quiet spot and dream about what it looks like to be free of this sin. Could freedom, peace, health, purity, patience, or love be on the other side? What is God telling you will be at the other side waiting for you? Discover the word with Jesus, then find a positive verse to match the word to encourage you to continue past these six weeks. Use the Internet, a concordance, or ask a Christian friend for a verse to match your word. Know that God wants you to succeed with this thing because He has brought you to it to watch you succeed.

May the Lord and the process be with you.

Signed, Leola and Veronica

This week has been quite an exciting week. We have been praying without ceasing for two weeks for these women, and God is answering our prayers. We have been praying for Dory too. We knew something was going on, but would not have even guessed it was what it was. My "intuitive antenna" had gone up a few times when talking with Dory, but I also had a feeling about her snooping too. I am so pleased to have this resolved for both of our sakes.

Veronica and I spent some time talking about week three after we ate our lunch. We cannot believe the amazing things God is doing, and it was only lunchtime. This weekend is going to be a weekend of joy, a stark difference from last weekend.

5
WISDOM BEHIND KNOWING

After a relaxing weekend, I got excited about the coming week. Veronica and I discussed my grand idea and we made arrangements for her to see the office downstairs on the very same day God gave me the idea. I explained what I would like to do, upon her agreement, while we ate our lunch one week ago today. We had thought we would have to cram all five of our clients into our office. I smiled at the idea of cramming them into this office. There is barely enough room for Veronica and I to stand at the same time, let alone seven of us. Thank the Lord, He is always on the job. We went down to their office to give Veronica a tour. Just as I had hoped, she loved it, and she loved Tabitha, Fabio, and Willie too. God's plan was falling into place much better than we had ever planned it.

Tabitha is tall and slim, yet muscular with a wonderfully booming personality. She was the first one to greet us as we walked through the side door. Her shoulder-length, mousey blonde hair looks exceptional on her. It is curly and frizzy at the same time, like mine, except mine is red. Her unruly hair goes well with the retro clothes she wears. She looks very comfortable inside her own boots, hair and all. I love that about her, considering she is an Occasion Organizer. I can just imagine what her events are like. If we ever have a fundraising event, Tabitha will be the one we hire to plan it. I like her.

Fabio has a broad chest with short legs and short brown hair. His muscles bulge out of his t-shirt, molding his sleeves into the creases of his arms rather than their natural position. It is obvious he trains himself as much as he trains his clients. He is soft-spoken, which is the complete opposite of his powerful physique. Both Veronica and I were pleasantly surprised by how articulate he is. He speaks using the finest of words with the tenderness of Jesus. No wonder he has so many clients. I suspected most of his clients were women, but I was wrong. He has set a "burly boundary" regarding his work with women. He will only train women at a public gym or as a husband/wife team. He knows a lot of personal trainers get themselves into serious trouble if they do not set these types of boundaries before they begin with their clients. Fabio wears his wedding ring, and when he is training he hangs it on his necklace for everyone to see. He is not ashamed to be married; as a matter of fact, he is darn proud of it. We know this because we talked about our workshop dealing with boundaries while explaining our plan. I am sure he would not have told us for any other reason. We were grateful for his honesty and impressed by his prior planning. It is good to know that there are men in the world today who hold themselves accountable for their own actions.

Then there is Willie, short for Willamina. She loves her whole name, but so many people say "Willee-a-Meena", adding an undesirable accent to it, that she shortened it to make it easier for them and for her ears. She was sitting behind her computer, writing an article for a magazine, when we introduced her to Veronica. She had a deadline, so she continued to work while we discussed the plan. She amazed me with her attentiveness to us and to her work at the same time. Her long, curly, auburn hair was pinned up using one of those leather clips with a stick through it. It looked like a clip my friend used in high school. Her hair was loose in the morning when I first visited and up when we came back. She said she always puts it up when she works so it does not get in the way of her typing. Willie always smiles when she talks, no matter what she is talking about. I like her because she is someone who can understand my writing blocks and can help me through it when I am writing workshops and my blog. She promised to be available for me, and I appreciate her offer.

We spend an hour with them, discussing what would become a very lucrative arrangement between the five of us and this building. We agreed to make the building a free-range building for everyone, yet our home base would remain our home bases, along with our privacy as well. We created a schedule online and added events to it, beginning with Thursday at 1 o'clock. We are more than willing to work downstairs so they can use our office, and they are more than willing to use our office while we utilize their space for our work. They also gave us a sample of a coffee from the "Frappe Mocha Smoka Machine". It was super delish! I cannot wait to offer our clients a bit of this tastiness on Thursday.

I know our plan for Thursday is from God because I feel at peace with the whole idea. I also think Gladys, Dee, Mary, Nicole, and Dory will like it too, but we need to be sensitive with our approach to grouping women together who have been working independently thus far. Up until last week, they had been able to keep their work to themselves, as well as their sin. Our goal in this plan is to allow them to have the support in each other, as well as us. 1 Peter 3:7-8[14] tells us to be like-minded and support each other. I believe each one of us is called to whatever we are going through so that we can

---

[14] 1 Peter 3:7-8 Finally, all *of you be* of one mind, having compassion for one another; love as brothers, *be* tenderhearted, *be* courteous; not returning evil for evil or reviling for reviling, but on the contrary blessing, knowing that you were called to this, that you may inherit a blessing.

have the blessing of helping each other get through what each of us is called to go through. Our God is so wonderful to give us each other, and I am of the mind we need to take advantage of this blessing to know each other and to love each other. Veronica and I want our clients to receive the blessing of knowing they are not alone.

We are blessed to have so many clients. We are creative and meticulous about the work God is giving us. He is in charge of this business, and we allow Him to guide us through every teaching. We do not stop pondering our message when we teach it; as a matter of fact, we continue to ponder and pray about it for the sake of our clients. We make sure we fully understand each one of our concepts. We ask one simple question every time – will this work for us? We have been observing these five clients working out the same basic sin based on their daily decisions. These decisions have been holding them back from many things, mainly from the peace of God. Each one of them has a habit controlled by the cravings of their body. I ponder this while drinking my Monday morning coffee. God is pointing me toward a verse to bring our body into submission. I reached for my Bible and my concordance to look it up. 1 Corinthians 9:27[15] tells us to bring our body into subjection. It seems to me that Jesus is asking us to offer up our body to Him for a reason. It is our actions that prove we trust God. Our actions can qualify us or disqualify us.

As I pondered this verse and our clients together, I began to see the link in every one of their experiences with God. God has asked us to offer our body to Him because it is His temple,[16] yet we have to keep its cravings under

---

[15] 1 Corinthians 9:27 But I discipline my body and bring it into subjection, lest, when I have preached to others, I myself should become disqualified.

[16] 1 Corinthians 6:19-20 Or do you not know that your body is the temple of the Holy Spirit who is in you, whom you have from God, and you are not your own? For you were bought at a price; therefore glorify God in your body and in your spirit, which are God's.

subjection. God has given us five senses that allow us to experience our world, but allowing those senses to control our actions is what gets us into trouble. For Gladys Pender, her sight causes her to spend money, and every time she saw something she liked, she had to have it. For Dee Zurtaker, her sense of taste goes into overload when she eats sweets, and her body craves them constantly. Mary Touchier's sense of touch is very important to her feeling of love; without it, she does not feel loved. Nicole Teen is a smoker who loves the smell of cigarettes and was drawn to them so she would have something to do with her hands. Dory MacIntyre's sense of hearing caused her great insecurities, leading her to gossip so she could feel superior to what she was currently feeling.

Veronica had come into the office, poured herself a coffee, and turned on her computer before I discovered she was even in the room. "Oh, my gosh! When did you get here?"s

"About ten minutes ago," she said, laughing. "An atom bomb could have dropped while you were thinking over there and you still would not have noticed. I envy you that focus."

"I was thinking about Thursday and how to help these women even more. Do you know what God has revealed to me? All of those ladies are having problems with controlling their senses. Gladys her sight, Dee her taste, Mary touch, Nicole smell, and Dory her hearing. This is not to say they have control of their other senses, but this is what they have sought us out to help them with. I wonder if we should address this on Thursday, so in the future they know what to look for," I said, with my typical thinking face. "I really think it is an excellent time to bring them together, because each of them is a great example of how we lose control of each of our senses independently and how much our ignorance of this can cause us to fall into all kinds of sin." I explained a synopsis of what I had been thinking about when she came into the office.

I think God brings me to information differently than

most people, based on the gifts He has bestowed upon me for His service. I grapple with information because I need to fully understand exactly what I know, and Jesus gives me information continuously because He knows I need to understand what is on my mind. For me, it is "out of sight, out of mind", so if it is important to me, I need to keep it in my sight. Thinking about it is keeping it in my sight. Senses spent the next couple of days churning in my mind.

We made sure our calendar for Wednesday afternoon was empty to discuss Thursday afternoon and what we hoped would happen with the gathering of the women. This would be the first group we joined together, and we pray there will be an opportunity to do it again if this one goes well. Typically, we work individually with each woman and give her a plan for her particular hardship. We have not had the great opportunity we do now with this group of women.

Thursday morning came with great anticipation for us. We gathered all of our paperwork together and brought it downstairs. Tabitha was in the office, making sure we had a perfectly clean place to meet with these ladies. This was our first swap. While we are downstairs, Willie is meeting with a new client at my desk, so I had to tidy it up as well. I have set a new boundary of never leaving my desk messy when I walk away from it. Since my hands were full and I was watching my feet, I had not noticed the new red and white plaid curtains on the wall. I put the load down on the counter by the "Frappe Mocha Smoka Machine". I looked up and immediately my eyes were drawn to the curtains. "Do not tell me! You didn't?" I ran over to them and pulled them open and there it was, "HeBoard Lower". I jumped up and down. I was so excited by their addition. I ran over and hugged Tabitha and told her to thank Willie and Fabio. I am so excited. This helps me to be able to make explanations to the women with drawings. "Oh, Jesus, You are so good. Thank You so much for providing for us wherever we go. I thank Jesus for you three," I said out loud.

Veronica told Tabitha, "We are going upstairs to eat

lunch, then we will come back down to get ready. The women will come to our office upstairs, so I will send them down here one at a time. We are very excited because this will be the first time we do this. We are praying it will be successful with this group, then when we run into the same situation we can do this again. Thank you so much for allowing this to happen and for putting up the board. We appreciate it." Veronica started walking to the door; I hugged Tabitha again and we went upstairs.

Lunch was over and we prayed for the coming hours to go peacefully and to be filled with the wisdom of God. I went downstairs while Veronica stayed upstairs to meet the women. Her instructions were to send them downstairs one at a time, and that is exactly what she did. I sat at one table, and when Dory came down, she sat with me. I moved to another table so when Nicole came down she sat with me, and I did that until all the women were sitting in different seats away from each other. Veronica came down and we started making coffee in the "Frappe Mocha Smoka Machine". When a foamy massiveness of hot sugar was sitting in front of each one of them, we began.

I started, because I am passionate about get-togethers. "Good afternoon, ladies. We believe there is wisdom in numbers, but more so, we believe people sharpen each other.[17] This is why we are all sitting in the same room today. Where two or more are gathered in His name, He is present,[18] and we need Jesus more than anything else for answers because He is the Answer," I said as I looked around. I had their attention, so I continued, "We have not revealed any information about you to each other, and none of you had advance knowledge that we were planning to meet as a group. We have sat you in different areas because you may want to

---

[17] Proverbs 27:17 As iron sharpens iron, so a man sharpens the countenance of the his friends.

[18] Matthew 18:20 For where two or three are gathered together in My name, I am there in the midst of them.

work alone, but we would prefer that you come together. Working together will make you stronger."

Veronica moved over to "HeBoard Lower" to open the curtains and get out the colour markers. "As you know, I am a week ahead of you, so we will use my week four list to show you what we are asking you to do this week. By using your journaling in week one and the lists from week two and three, we will begin to discern what we need to do to be successful obeying God to eliminate this sin." On one side of the board she began copying from her journal and lists, while the women got their own books out.

I began to give instructions. "The first three weeks you have been gathering information to make you aware of how your life had been wrapped around this thing God has asked you to stop because it is sin to Him. God said you shall have no gods before Him,[19] and He has asked you to eliminate this god you have set up for yourself. The god you have set up is your own body. Each one of you is allowing one of the senses, belonging to your body, to control your actions. I would like permission to tell you which sense that is for each of you." This premise intrigued me, and I could see by their faces they were intrigued too, as each of them were nodding their head. "I will start with Dory, the sense in control for you is hearing. For Gladys, it is sight. For Nicole, it is smell." She nodded her head knowingly, "For Dee, it is taste," another nod, "and for Mary, touch."

This was something that brought them together because they understood how similar their troubles were. Now I know exactly why God brought me to this idea. I silently said a "thank You, Jesus" quickly and continued. "Last week, every one of you was attempting to stop your sin with Jesus. Do you have your chart? How did it go?"

Dory started, "You were right about my hearing. I should let you all know that I gossip." She looked around at everyone with a sad face to let them know she was not happy

---

[19] Exodus 20:3 You shall have no other gods before Me.

with herself. "Every time I hear about someone who is doing better than me, I berate myself and berate them by gossiping about them. I have alienated all of my family and my neighbours too, except Leola and Veronica. They have been very kind to me, even though they had heard all about me saying those nasty things to people. I forgot to mention that I live next door, and it is seeing you women come and go with smiles that brought me here. To answer your question, Leola, I did try to stop, but was mostly unsuccessful this week. I called out to Jesus to help me, and I heard in my spirit to stop talking and just listen. Jesus knows how hard that is for me, but I will attempt it. I at least know what my goal is now. I think I know what my promise from God is, but I would still like to pray about it some more, if you don't mind."

"Absolutely. Thank you, Dory. Would someone else like to tell us how they did?" Veronica asked. I like that Dory just steps in to talk.

We looked around for a couple of seconds of dead air when Nicole stood up. "I also think you are right about my sense of smell being my god. I love the smell of cigarette smoke, so every time I tried to quit before, when I smelled smoke I craved a cigarette and began smoking again. This week, I actually tried to quit smoking for one day, but I was not successful because I smelled smoke. Again this week I have gained some very good information I did not have before that I believe will add to the hope I already have to be successful." She sat down with a huge smile on her face. Her excitement kept the ladies testifying.

"I called on Jesus every morning to stop me from spending because I know that everything I see I have to have. Last week God taught me how He was going to stop me from purchasing something I was not supposed to buy, so this week I paid very close attention to what He was doing in my body, but I still purchased stuff I do not need nor did I even want. I feel like God is using my body against me to cure me of this." Gladys admitted this with her head down. She feels shame for not being able to stop this. "I think it should be simple to stop shopping, but it is hard. Apparently, I am still bored, but I am beginning to do more volunteer work; maybe it just is not the right work."

"Thank you, Gladys." I said, "I am impressed with what you all have learned this past week. Information will always get you closer to success."

Dee spoke this time. "I love desserts." Everyone looked at her in amazement because of her slight size, but that did not stop them from nodding in agreement. "I was trying very hard this week to stop them, but I have been in the habit for so long that my body craves them every day. I also cried out to Jesus for help with this too. He was silent, and I have come to the conclusion that He spoke but my ears are closed. I might be having a problem with obedience." She sat down with a disparaging plop. I feel for her. I have been there and done that too.

"I cannot let Dee end on that note. I am having a problem with obedience too. I hate not touching people. It hurts my feelings that God would even ask me to stop touching people. I love Jesus, but I still don't understand why I have to depend on a non-physical God to satisfy my need to be touched. I am obeying Him, but I do not like it." Mary confessed, with hurt in her voice.

I suspect each one of them has had issues with God at one time or another, based on a lack of understanding of God's plan for them. We think our life is going along perfectly fine when God steps in to ask us to do something that makes no sense to us at the time. His ways are not our ways, and His thoughts are not our thoughts,[20] until we know Him well enough to know what He is doing. He is more than willing to tell us what He is doing, but He will not do it until we learn to obey Him. When He tells us to do something, we need faith to do it. I knew exactly what they are going through emotionally, because I have felt everything they are feeling.

---

[20] Isaiah 55:8-9

"Thank you so much, all of you, for testifying so truthfully. Bringing you together was God's idea, and He knows exactly what He is doing with each one of us individually and together. Now that Veronica has her work done on the board, we will begin talking about the great work we will be doing for next Thursday. You can move closer together, if you would like." I said to them.

The ladies started getting up one by one to sit by each other. They shook each other's hands and pulled chairs around the table closest to "HeBoard Lower". In a few minutes, all five of them were sitting at one table. I smiled. Veronica put all of the markers on the table she had dragged closer to her. She arranged them in order while we watched. She put the colours in the order of the rainbow. I am not sure if anyone else noticed, but I did, and to me that was a sign these women would be perfectly fine under the care of our God. I smiled again, looked up, and said a silent "Thank You".

"We are going into week four and we will let you write these notes in your journal, as you understand them. We have a printout for you with these words, and examples too." This is the printout we gave them, and we read it word for word to them, plus gave them examples from the board.

Week 4: Wisdom Week

I believe there is wisdom and accountability in numbers. *Where two or more are gathered in His name He is present.*[21] You need Jesus more than anything else to solve these problems. Working together with other women who love Jesus and are like-minded will make you stronger.

Having someone to talk with who is going through the same trials you are is very comforting and allows you to have an accountability partner. I want you to be able to comfort each other as you go through this. Paul says in 2 Corinthians

---

[21] Matthew 18:20

1:4 that the Father *comforts us in all our tribulation, that we may be able to comfort those who are in any trouble, with the comfort with which we ourselves are comforted by God.*

You are learning this week the wisdom behind knowing what makes you tick. You are still journaling using the directives from the previous weeks. Keep the charts going if you are adding new discoveries, but if you are repeating the same thing each week, having it in your chart once is enough. You will copy from your journaling what you need to do to be successful in eliminating these things that lead to your transgression. On a clean sheet of paper, write a list of every transgression you have committed, from week one to week three. Below on the left is Veronica's clean sheet list of things she did from her journal.

List from Veronica's Journal	**List from Veronica's Journal**
Yelled obscenities in my car	~~Yelled obscenities in my car~~
Repeated no's	Repeated no's
Told my truth	Told my truth
Bullied someone	~~Bullied someone~~
Voiced my dislike of someone	~~Voiced my dislike of someone~~
Returned mean talk	~~Returned mean talk~~
Rolled my eyes at someone	Rolled my eyes at someone
Silent treatment	Silent treatment
	Mean talk to hurt

Once your list is done, go through it to eliminate similar subjects and create a new one that speaks to the ones you've eliminated. From Veronica's list above on the left, join "yelled obscenities, bullied someone, voiced my dislike, and returned mean talk" together to make "mean talk to hurt", knowing that when you do these things you hurt someone. You can cross those joined subjects out on your list and add a new subject called "mean talk to hurt" at the bottom of the list (see the above list on the right).

Easiest to Hardest to Eliminate List

1. Repeated No's
2. Told my truth
3. Silent treatment
4. Bad body language
5. Mean talk to hurt

   Using your new list, number each item starting from one (being easy to eliminate) to the last one being hardest to eliminate. Rewrite the list again in order (see side list). Write every one of them, regardless of the number of subjects. Whatever it takes for you to eliminate this sin is perfectly fine with Jesus. He is more interested in the elimination of the subject, especially if He is requiring it of you. Have your list ready for week five.
   May the Lord and the process be with you.
Signed, Leola and Veronica

   We instructed them to continue journaling and trying to eliminate their transgressions, making note of any new issues. They also will continue talking to Jesus about it, and I had one more thing Jesus had given me for them. "The Lord spoke to me this week while I was in my personal reading time in His Word. He wanted me to give each of you a verse to memorize, and of course He gave me the verses for you, so if they set your spirit on fire, He is responsible. Gladys, He gave me James 5:7 for you. I expect that you will look these verses up and memorize them how you do that best. I can give you some "how to" clues, but what I do may not work for you. The verse God gave me for Dee is Ezekiel 2:8, and for you, Mary, Esther 5:2. Nicole, your verse is Isaiah 3:24, and for you, Dory, Ezekiel 2:10. These verses made perfect sense to me, but for you they may not mean anything yet. Memorize them anyway."
   Veronica began to speak, "Did you bring your pictures?" Each woman got them out, and I collected them while

Veronica continued. "If you have not received God's promised word to you, pray again this week. because next week you will need that word. God has chosen LOVE as my promise. When I have overcome negative talk, I will love better. God gave me Luke 6:31 to spur me on: *Do unto others as you would have them do unto you.* I do not like negative talk aimed at me, so I am going to change this for people so they do not have to listen to it from me. God also reminded me I am not alone, because in Revelation 2 there was a loveless church who needed to repent." Her face showed her grief for being negative.

"We will meet here again next Thursday at one o'clock with your journals. You are more than welcome to call and make an appointment to see either Veronica or myself to help with your list. If you would like to stay and chat with each other, you are more than welcome. We have half an hour with this office before we must leave. Would anyone like another one of those 'Frappe Strape Contrapes'?" They laughed at the name I gave it and all nodded emphatically, so off I went to go wrestle with that "Frappe Mocha Smoka Machine".

They stayed another twenty minutes to get to know one another. We listened to them laughing while we cleaned. A couple of them inquired if Veronica and I needed help, but we refused to allow them the time together. Once they left, Veronica and I hugged each other for support and congrats. This meeting went well for us, and for them. We prayed fervently that bringing these women together would be fruitful, and God answered us with a "yes". We thanked God for this office as well. We had been looking for a place to begin a Bible Study for women and now we had it.

Friday was a busy day as well. We decided to advertise "Raising the White Picket Fence" as a "group workshop", and a local women's church group asked us to begin teaching it on Friday. We began week one this morning. After we finished instructing them, we came back to the office to unwind. Going over this information with one woman at a time was much easier than twenty-four. It is a good thing we required two hours per week to teach, because it takes that long to get everyone in the same mind. One of Andrew's lunches was going to come in handy, because we talked so much about how to improve our communication skills that we forgot to stop for lunch.

When we walked into our office, Tabitha was sitting at my desk. "Hiya. I didn't see you on the schedule for today, or did I miss it?" It didn't seem like she was working anyway. I continued to walk to the other side of my desk to drop my bag down on the floor beside my guest chair. I plopped down into it. I am not usually a "plopper", but today I made an exception.

"I saw in the schedule you would be gone, so I came up to sit in your office. This morning when I came into my office, I felt something different I had not felt before. I wondered what it was, then I remembered you had used our office yesterday with your clients. Do not worry, you left it the way you found it." She smiled, "there is just something different about the atmosphere down there now, and I wanted to see if that same atmosphere is up here. It is. You brought something into this building that was not here before. I am now sure it is the Spirit of God," she said, looking straight into my eyes.

"I bring Him with me wherever I go, because He is inside me and He can be inside you too," I said with a smile.

"I don't know if I am ready for that, but I can notice the difference in our whole office now. I saw Dory today and she didn't even bother me. Typically, I cannot even look at her without getting angry, but she has changed, and I can feel it. She even apologized to me for being nosy. I do not have a church-going family, so I do not know anything about this, but I am going to do some research. Anyway, I have an appointment with a client in twenty minutes, so I better get going. Have a good weekend and see you next week." She blew her curly hair out of her eyes and got up from my desk. Those few freckles around her nose and cheeks gave her a youthful look, but I would guess her to be in her late thirties or early forties, although she dresses like she is in her twenties.

We ended the day with a prayer for the women, one for us and one for the folks downstairs, mentioning Tabitha by name. She is seeking God and we know God is at work in her. We are going to mind our own business and let God do His work, because we are not evangelists; we specialize more in discipleship. God has gifted us to teach women to grow in their faith and their knowledge of God while using that information and knowledge to improve their life skills. The Bible is the Book of Life we use as our guide to train women in both their skills for life and for growth. We are happy to do just that every day, because it makes us grow in our faith and knowledge of our Saviour. No day is a good day without increasing our knowledge of our Father.

6
FORTIFY YOURSELF

I love having my Monday morning coffee, staring out the window, talking to Jesus. I praise Him over and over for the wonderful work He is doing in our clients' lives and the work He is doing in Veronica and I as well. The days are screaming by, and soon the women we work with will be able to study the Bible for themselves to find God's way out of their sin. This is the task laid out to us by God, but I can foresee this being emotionally difficult when they leave our tutelage. I am going to fall in love with each woman and miss her terribly when I am not seeing her again. I just know I am going to cry when bidding them farewell. In the fall, we will begin the "Precepts and Promises Bible Study", but we know some of them will not be able to attend. These women are getting help because they cannot find God's way on their own, but when they can find it, their life will be different and they will fall in line with the plan God has for them. Their plan may not include our Bible study. This is the sad part about our task and the great part about our God. He allows us to help Him train these women so we can set them free into His hands and under His wings. I thank God every day for this great opportunity.

God has opened some astonishing doors and we expect, as long as we allow the Holy Spirit to lead our clients to Christ, more will open. There is no other Name to save them from themselves and no other Book to show them how. Veronica and I are living proof of that. I gave the women their personal verses, just as Jesus has always given me mine. It was such a joy to be a part of the things God is doing in their lives. Dory, Gladys, Dee, Nicole, and Mary seemed to honestly enjoy each other's company while providing information into their life they most likely had never told anyone else. They told each other a lot of information in the short twenty minutes they had together. They each talked about their family and how God has been working in their life. Mary took on the leadership role as soon as I walked away. She told a fact and asked each lady to tell a fact. She works in the children's ministry at her church and brought those skills right into this gathering.

"You look far from this world," Tabitha said as she came in the office. I screamed like a scared rabbit. "I have been standing here for about two minutes watching you. You smiled, then you frowned, then you smiled again. What were you thinking about?"

What I am thinking is I should lock the door in the morning to avoid the embarrassing scream I have. "Well darlin', you scared the devil out of me. Good morning. Grab a coffee, coffee. We don't have 'frappe mocha smoka' coffee, just coffee, coffee." I smiled, "I was thinking about how God has done such wonderful things this last week and every week since we opened Crown for Life. I love the job God has given me to do."

"What is that exactly?" she asked, looking at me with one eyebrow up. "I call myself an 'Occasion Organizer' because 'Event Planner' is too plain and popular. What do you call yourself?"

"I am 'The Biblical Life Skills Strategist'. God gave me that name eight years ago. I started teaching secular life skills workshops in 2005, but I renamed myself to 'The Biblical

Life Skills Strategist' about two years ago because God allowed it. I will continue to teach non-Christian workshops as well, although each workshop is designed with information I garnered from the Bible, which I call the 'Book of Life'."

"God gave you the name and the task?" I nodded my head as she continued talking, "I wanted to talk to you about that too." Tabitha said as she sat down across from me. "How do you know when God is talking to you?" she put a twenty-dollar bill, to pay for the questions, in front of me and I slid it back to her.

"He talks to me in multiple ways. First and always, He talks to me when I read the Bible, which I will commonly refer to as His Word." I tapped the top of my Bible on my desk. "He also talks to me using someone else's voice, and He nudges me. The nudges are repeated pushes toward a specific direction that are aimed directly at us personally. When God wanted me to stop gossiping, He made me feel bad every time I said something negative about someone. When God wants you to do something, His Spirit will convict you in a manner that speaks directly to you personally. No two people are the same, therefore the Holy Spirit speaks to each one of us differently. It is only by reading the Bible that we can learn how to follow His leading and if it truly is Him, because the devil can do all those things to us too. It is extremely important we know the difference."

She looked at me as she thought about that. "How did you know it was Him before you started reading the Bible? I always thought Christians were either stuffy or insane. Never did I think they are anything like you. You and Veronica have fun, and I honestly think you enjoy life."

"I do not know how you are feeling, but for me, it was a leading to find a church. I felt like I was missing something if Sunday went by and I had not searched out a church to attend." I smiled. "I found a church but did not stay. I was without for a time, but God kept nudging me, so I asked my friend where she went. I attended her church and have never looked back. This is not about the church building, it is about you and God. But to become a mature Christian, you will find being with other Christians serves to assist with your knowledge of God." I pointed to the Bible on my desk.

Tabitha smiled at me, "Ironic enough that I was looking online for a church yesterday. I could not choose, so I stayed home. What I really wanted to do was just come here and soak up what it is that is in here." She looked puzzled.

"Let me tell you a story about Saul. Jesus called him in a peculiar way[22] on his way to murder Christians. Saul was a Jew bent on doing the work of God, but Jesus stepped in." I pulled my Bible close. "After his conversion, Paul went to Arabia to learn from Jesus Himself for three years.[23] If God is just calling you to wait, then do that. He will teach you by Himself what He wants you to do. Do you have a Bible?"

She smiled a big smile. "I thought I heard God tell me to buy a Bible, so I went to a Christian bookstore in Windsor on Saturday to ask for help with picking one out. They were good at asking me the right questions to see what style I would like to read. I had no idea there were so many styles and versions."

"You can get free online Bibles too. I utilize them all the time, although I like the paper Bible best. I colour in it, write in it, and underline verses. I would like to tell you something I wish I had done from the beginning. Underline verses that highlight the promises of God and do your best to avoid underlining negative verses reminding you of the bad things you do. God wants us to realize the good He has created us to be, not dwell on the bad we are now." There is so much I wanted to tell her, but I refrained and opened the Bible instead to let it speak for itself.

Tabitha purchased a New King James Version, my favourite. I told her to use an online Bible too because she can change the version of Bible she reads if she needs understanding, plus she knows she can call me or come up

---

[22] Acts 9
[23] Galatians 1:11-12, 15-18

any time she wants to discuss what she is learning. I invited her to the church I attend next Sunday, and she accepted. I also invited her to attend the "Precepts and Promises Bible Study" we are beginning in September. She got up to go downstairs at the same time that Veronica came in. Again, Veronica was carrying a bag of food prepared by her husband. This is her Monday morning ritual. Tabitha opened the door for her and disappeared. I got up to help.

Eating these lunches is resulting in a weight gain for me, so I decided to eat half at a time and forgo the afternoon snack to see how that goes. If I continue to gain weight, I will ask Andrew to make my portions smaller or start making my own lunch. My problem is that I am eating while my mind is somewhere else. When I do that, I definitely overeat. While I was thinking about that, I heard my name.

"Leola!" Veronica laughed at me for "zoning out" while I work. "What did Tabitha want? Does she need our office today?"

"No. She had some questions about God." I said, smiling.

"Really. What did she want to know?"

I told her what we talked about as we put the rest of the food away. I also told her about my plan to lose the extra pounds I've been packing on, because I lack portion control of this deliciousness we are putting away. I want to start either going out for a bike ride at noon or for a walk. I am in need of making sure I am healthy enough to keep doing this work for years to come. Plus, exercise tends to clear my mind. This is only the beginning, and God's plan for this work will only get bigger. I do not want to be too sick to do it, so I have some of my own boundaries to set. I don't think we ever grow out of setting boundaries because we never stop catering to our bodies. Our body tells us when it needs help, and we need to answer. Our senses can lead us into all kinds of ungodly situations if we allow it, but our mind needs to get control of those senses. Every one of my senses is activated with this food, but it is time to tell them what they should be

THE PICKET WHITE FENCE

seeing, hearing, touching, smelling, and tasting, not the other way around.

I rode my bike to work on Tuesday since I live close, and put my clothes in my backpack, along with some supplies to make myself presentable. I thank God for the ability to shower at work. Since my husband and I moved to LaSalle twenty years ago, I can ride my bike to work and it will only taken me ten minutes to get here. Our office and my house are close to the new highway leading to the Gordy Howe Bridge to the United States, including 22 kilometers of fantastic trail. I chose to take a ride along the trails before heading to work to extend my exercise. There are a lot of hills, valleys, and bridges to cross where I rode, which gives me a decent workout and shaky legs.

I had to haul my bike up the steps because I forgot my lock at home. When I got to the top of the stairs I opened the door and just left my bike at the top, leaning against the railing. I got the coffee pot brewing, locked the door, and got into the shower. God speaks to me while I am in the shower, because it is a place no one else can be with me. I was thinking about Thursday's workshop. We went to the store to buy all the supplies and now we have to cut and paste. This is going to be fun, but I want to make sure we have enough supplies cut out. We have some new clients coming today, but we are going to start after we are finish with them this afternoon.

Shower done and coffee in hand, I head to my desk to take in the view out the window and talk with Jesus. I left home a little early so I could do all I needed to do and still have time to read the Bible and pray. I have to take time to know Jesus every day, because if I do not, I feel lost. This was one thing I really had to set burly boundaries around. I can get side tracked easily at my house with kids and TV. It was important for me to know God, so I did it. I can tell in everyone's life what is important to them, not by what they say, but by what they do. Boundaries help us to make sure we are doing what we say we want to do. It is as simple as that and as hard as that.

I prayed for all of the women who are working on the "Raising the White Picket Fence" workshop. I petitioned God to give them strength, to not only finish what they started, but to begin anew after understanding how successful they will be when they learn this well. Every goal deserves to be surrounded by boundaries. As I sat drinking my coffee, I was reminded of the many different kinds of boundaries God and I discussed. I am all about naming things so we can remember them, so I can remember them. I also like to have fun with the teachings I give as well, so I will rhyme, or have them all the same letter, or use synonyms. This is not to take away the importance of boundary setting and defending. I know full well if not for the boundaries I set, I would not have reached any goal or been able to do anything God called me to do. I make things quirky so we can remember easier while having fun working on them.

Veronica walked in, but this time, I heard the ding. I had been going over some information about tomorrow's gathering on "HeBoard" when I heard the ding. Seems I hear the ding when I am writing on the board, but not when I am sitting at my desk. It is peculiar, to say the least, but not worth thinking about. I closed the curtains until I saw Veronica's face in the window, then I opened them back up. I had jotted down the types of boundaries and was pondering how to effectively relay their meanings. Veronica sat at her desk and joined in on the conversation. We discussed how to make each definition small but powerful. We completed three of the five when we heard the ding. I closed the curtains and began the day with our new clients.

With our clients gone, I opened up "Heboard" again. We needed to get this done so we could start putting together the packages for each of the five ladies. We discussed them more and came up with a sound list with excellent definitions. While I was writing, Veronica was typing to add the new definitions to the handouts for tomorrow. We then cut and coloured the pieces, which took us right up until it was time to leave. Veronica took her supplies home to make her fence for show-and-tell. I am going to make mine with them. I was pooped and forgot I rode my bike. Shoot, do I take the trail or the road? How can I look myself in the face if the very first day I ride my bike to work I skimp out and take the low road? To the trail I went, with the power of Christ in me.

    I have been excited for this day since we started teaching about boundaries. This is my favourite part of the whole workshop. Once I finished my shower, on this fine Thursday morning, I started cutting and organizing. We collected pictures from them last week, so I attached them to their personal "Fence Raising Kit", for presentation only. They are going to use the picture elsewhere. We bought a roll of magnetic tape, Bristol board, and coloured construction paper. I am a visual person, and I think a lot more people are than we think. Oh, let's be real, I do this for me because I love creating visual aids. Visual people need visual aids to learn, and I am more than happy to accommodate. We bought baskets for each item, plus one with pens, markers, glue, and scissors. My husband came to install shelves for us to store our baskets. This is going to be fun once we explain what to do.

    One o'clock came like lightning. We had the office set-up with everything they needed to be successful. We put three tables together so we would have room for all of us to sit down together. Veronica stuck her fence on "HeBoard Lower", along with writing all of her list as examples. I will create my board with them to banish my love handles. Veronica started week five's discussion with the list from last week's work.

    "Does everyone have their list complete?"

    Dee spoke first. "I think my list is too long, so can you help me make it smaller? I am sure I can reword it better to make it shorter." And a couple more of them nodded their heads in agreement. We spent the first half hour rewriting all of their lists to suit them better, then we helped them think about numbering them easiest to hardest. To help them with that, I asked them a question, "Which one of these causes you to cringe the most? That one is your last one, then eliminate by "cringe factor" until you have one left. That one will be your easiest; not that any of them will be easy." It is time for a sugar break. We also brought coffee, coffee down for Mary and I, because that sugar is not on my menu anymore.

Veronica opened the curtains on "HeBoard Lower" to reveal this week's project. "In the baskets are the supplies you will need to 'Raise the White Picket Fence'. You may not get it finished before you leave, and this is okay. You can take the supplies you need home and finish there. We provided you with a 'Fence Raising Kit' to carry your supplies and white board home." We handed out the kits, and I moved to the board.

"Pull out your magnetic white board from your 'Fence Raising Kit'. Find your picture and unattach it from your bag. Set your board in front of you and your numbered list. I hope you have your word this week, because you absolutely need it now. I am going to join you in making a 'White Picket Fence' on a board, because this tummy is not supposed to be here. My word is healthy." I gave them each a look to see if they had their word and they all did. "This is what you are going to make." I pointed to Veronica's fence on "HeBoard Lower". "This is the 'White Picket Fence' that will help you be who you want to be. The first 'Foundational Post' will have your picture on it and the last 'Foundational Post' will have you becoming your word."

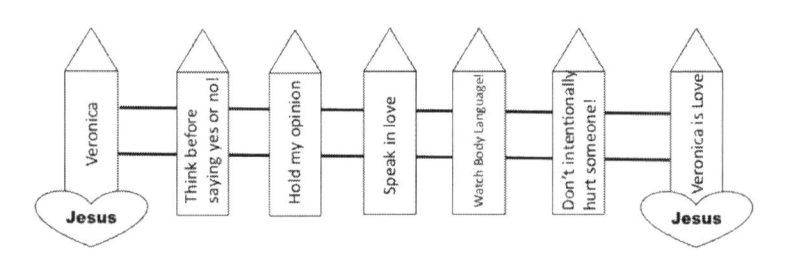

| Jesus — Veronica — Think before saying yes or no! — Hold my opinion — Speak in love — Watch Body Language! — Don't intentionally hurt someone! — Veronica is Love — Jesus |

I saw a little smile on their faces based on the look of the fence, then as quick as it came, it disappeared. "Do not worry, we are going to walk you through this," I said with confidence. "You will know how to raise your own 'White Picket Fence' when we are finished." I brought the baskets of supplies to the table and handed out notes from the printer instead of handwritten this week. I began to read it with adlibbing.

Week 5 – Fortification Week

You cannot completely protect a boundary without knowing why you have created it. A fortified boundary is created with the full knowledge of why it exists. You are going to start this week by gaining an understanding of your boundaries before you set them up in your life. Your numbered list will turn into a set of boundaries to establish for yourself, with your Word as your goal. Listed below are five different types of boundaries you will set throughout your life from this day forward. Together, we will ponder your list of numbered boundaries to identify its boundary type. This will help you discern the magnitude of each boundary. If you need to renumber your boundaries based on this list, now is a good time to make that change.

1. *Brief Boundary*: A boundary designed to be temporary, for the use of cutting something out of your life for a short period of time that will impede your success, such as a weekly social outing or extra tasks. What you will cut out is not wrong, in and of itself, it is just impeding your success at this particular goal.

2. *Blanket Boundary*: A boundary designed to surround you for life. It never goes away and never stops being applied, such as not stealing or gossiping. This boundary usually starts out slow,

then picks up pace until it is applied to your life forever.

3. *Burly Boundary*: A boundary designed to help you avoid an identified desire that could lead you into sin at any time. This temptation could ruin you if it leads to sexual sin, dishonesty, drugs, alcohol, abuse, anger, or the like.

4. *Bouncing Boundary*: A boundary set today but is not utilized again until the temptation returns into your life. There may be a time when something was a heavy temptation for you (such as swearing) but is not anymore, although every so often you may need to utilize this particular boundary again.

5. *Banished Boundary*: A boundary set in the past that no longer applies to your life, because you have defended it with such vigor it is no longer a temptation for you, such as smoking, drinking, stealing, gossiping, or the like.

This week, you are going to learn how to fortify yourself with boundaries and what the result should be when you protect them. You have a list completed of your Personal Boundaries. We are going to use this list to build our fence using the supplies in the baskets.

Create the parts for your White Picket Fence

"You will need a 'New Foundational Post' and a 'Renewed Foundational Post', plus as many posts as you have numbers on your list. Get two posts, plus as many other posts as you need from the basket marked 'posts'. You also need a foundation for the 'New Foundational Post' and 'Renewed Foundational Post', because these posts need a firm foundation, which is Jesus. We have created hearts, because He loves us, for that foundation and wrote the Name of Jesus on them for you to use. We want a foundation based on love. These parts are what you are looking for in the baskets." I held up the post and the foundations we created for them.

Build your White Picket Fence.

"We are going to put them together as your 'White Picket Fence'. *Looking unto Jesus, the author and finisher of our faith* (Hebrews 12:2a). Your foundation must be Jesus, or you will not be successful defending your boundaries. Create your 'Foundational Posts' by attaching the Jesus shape to the bottom of two of your posts. Then, on one of the two 'Foundational Posts', attach your picture. This will be your 'New Foundational Post', because you are beginning anew to do what Jesus requires of you. On the 'Renewed Foundational Post', write your promised word, similar to Veronica's 'Renewed Foundational Post' on the board, 'Veronica is Love'. It is called 'renewed' because you are becoming renewed in your promise." We created our foundational posts, and Veronica took over.

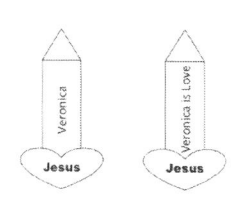

"Attach a magnet to the back of the foundational posts and affix them to your board beside each other, like I have on the board. The objective is to merge your foundational post, but there is something preventing you from doing that – your sins." Veronica said this with great sadness. She looked at her own fence, knowing how long it will take for her negative self to be merged with her loving self. We are all feeling this sadness. Then she speaks again, with hope in her words.

"We created these boundaries to help us be successful at merging with our word, so let us get started. Using your list, write each personal boundary on one post. Put a magnet on the rear of each of them. Starting with boundary number one beside your 'New Foundational Post', attach it to the board and keep attaching your posts in order until you get to the 'Renewed Foundational Post'. The 'Renewed Foundational Post' will always be your last post, and it remains stationary because you are walking toward this goal, it is not coming toward you. Draw lines with a dry erase marker, joining all of your posts together. You can look at my 'White Picket Fence' on the board for a visual of what your 'White Picket Fence' will resemble."

I had to pry myself away from my board to give them more instruction. "You have done a phenomenal job working on your board. This board is a reminder that you have established these personal boundaries in your life. Display your board, when complete, in a place of prominence to remind you of each of your boundaries and the need to defend them. Defending them means that you will do them or abide by them." I wanted to make sure they understood what I meant by defending their boundaries. They did.

"To add more power to your Boundary Board this week, you will need to find an encouraging verse to go along with your promised Word from God. This week, spend some time with God, as well as searching the Bible for a verse that suits your promise. God chose Luke 6:31 for Veronica's board, and I am sure you will be able to find one just as poignant. Write it in your journal and bring it with you next week." I told them they could stay and work on their boards for a little while.

We worked together until the time was up. Two hours goes by much quicker than I ever expect it will, yet when I am waiting at the dentist, it seems to take two days to go by. The ladies all left with completed fences and a renewed strength to be successful. I sat and looked at my completed fence. There is nothing better for me than to have a visual "in my face" way of attacking my goal. That is what is going to make their "White Picket Fence" become more of a successful adventure than those who just say, "I am going to stop doing such and such." They try their best to stick to it each day, but they fail because they have no plan to follow, just their empty words from a current frustration or a subsequent consequence.

    I am excited to see how this next week unfolds for them. They have been through three weeks of watching their behaviour and one week of actually staring at it to put it all together. They are learning a great deal about themselves and their behaviours. This week, they are going to take this plan they have created and use it to combat their sin to reach the goal God has set for them. The exciting part about this week, of course, is the plan. "Raising the White Picket Fence" is all about the plan. Boundaries are all about the plan. When there is no plan, we typically fail, but with a plan in place, especially with boundaries, it takes the thinking out of it and puts our plan into action. When faced with a choice, pre-planning our response will ensure we make the right choice each and every time. Our excitement about this plan to pre-plan was obvious to the ladies.

    We walked up the stairs on Thursday, exhausted yet exuberant. Tomorrow, our church group will tell us how their first full week has gone, tracking their behaviours, but for now, home is where I want to plunk these weary bones. As I rode my bike home, I thought about the first time God showed me how to set boundaries and defend them. I have grown exponentially since then in how I create them, why I create them, and how well I defend them. He has taught me so thoroughly how to do this that I count it all joy to come into hardship, knowing I can overcome it due to His teachings. I know He will be with me every single step through every single roadblock to every single mountaintop. God has made me who I am and continues to transform me into what He created me to be. I am eager to see who I will be tomorrow.

7
ENCOURAGE AND INSPIRE

Since I have been around this circle before losing weight, I have been able to set my boundaries without going through the process of documenting what I need to do to be successful. When you have been working this process for a long time, it gets easier each time you have to use it. That is where I am today. This valley is not new to me because I had previously lost ninety pounds, but over the years my weight has crept up to past my limit that I had set for twenty pounds. I struggled to figure out why the weight is going up but just recently found the answer – my step counter and heart rate monitor are not suited for me. I should have known this because I entered a body fat reduction contest once with a body fat machine that measured me with more body fat despite weight loss. I have some kind of electrical short in my body that messes with machines, so I am not going to use machines anymore and just reduce my calorie intake until the love handles are gone. I know tons of women have gone through this struggle as they aged. Unexplained weight gain and no one to explain how to get rid of it. I have just had to figure out what I am doing wrong on my own and learn more about my body than I used to know. Due to the fact I have been in this valley before, I am better equipped to handle it.

I thank God for Monday morning coffee. I don't take sugar or milk in my coffee, so that is one thing I have not had to eliminate. I rode my bike to work, took my shower, and am now sitting in front of the window in my second week of eating properly and riding my bike to work the long way. It gets easier in the third week, but the second week is usually the hardest for me. The first week I am running on adrenaline and that disappears in the second week, but I know if I get through it, I will be good. It is normally the second week that I relent and start filling my face with anything and everything. I typically keep up with the exercise but give up on the healthy eating. This time I am going to get through this second week to the third, then the fourth, and so on. As I sip my coffee, I am reminded that Jesus is the one who wants me healthy, not me. The bi-product of getting healthy is I can do God's work for longer, even into my eighties. Thinking about doing this until I am well into my eighties makes me smile. I imagine sitting in this window at the ripe old age of eighty-five, having my morning coffee and daydreaming about what we will do next for the women of Essex County. Will we still be in this office, or will we have our Life Skills Center opened with an office in there?

God has made me so hopeful as of late that now all I can think about is what He will do in the future with these women and us for trusting in Him so much that we put everything down before Him. We are putting our cigarettes, our sweets, our gossip, our health, our money, our negativity, and our need for love in front of the Cross, believing Jesus will not abandon us. We believe He will make us whole in this matter, which will make us stronger to deal with the next matter. We believe He will heal our wounds that are causing us to commit the sins that drag us down into the nearest gutter. We just simply believe He has the power to do whatever He wants to do, and we want that power living in us; therefore, we obey Him.

Just as we instructed our clients to do, I wrapped my "Boundary Board" in my Fence Kit bag and put it in my backpack Thursday night to bring home. I wanted to pray over it, to make sure I had burned my tasks into my head. I put my list together and created my "Boundary Board" just as everyone else did. I created a list of things that I am doing wrong daily that are leading me to gain weight. It starts with not getting enough cardiovascular exercise, going all the way to my eating habits and implementing weight lifting. I paid attention for a couple of days to see what I was doing, then I made an informed decision about what it took to make sure I am successful at getting rid of these extra twenty-five pounds. For the time being, I am going to bring my board to work and put it in the window as a reminder of my boundaries

Leola's Combined List		Leola's Boundary List
Use Body instead of driving	New Foundational Post	Leola
Cut portions in half	Posted Boundary #1	Walk/Bike more
Choose healthier foods	Posted Boundary #2	Eat 1300 Cal.
Eat fruit more	Posted Boundary #3	Fast from Sweets (6 Days)
Weight train 3 times per week	Posted Boundary #4	Weight Lift (3 days)
	Renewed Foundational Post	Leola is Healthy

Fence diagram with posts labeled left to right: Leola (Jesus heart), Walk/Bike More, Eat 1300 Cal., Fast from Sweets (6 Days), Weight Lift (3 days), Leola is Healthy (Jesus heart).

Or do you not know that your body is the temple of the Holy Spirit who is in you, whom you have from God, and you are not your own? For you were bought at a price; therefore glorify God in your body and in your spirit, which are God's. 1 Corinthians 6:19-20

As I was looking at my board, I heard the ding, then saw Tabitha. A week had gone by since I talked with her last. She walked over to my desk to look at my "Boundary Board". She just stood looking at it.

"Does God teach you this stuff, or do you come up with it on your own?" She was touching the posts and reading each one of them separately. She does not have a weight problem because Fabio would lecture her every day. She told me one time she went on vacation to return with a bit of a gut from over-indulging on the cruise, and Fabio mentioned it every chance he could until it was gone. Then, and only then, did he stop talking about it. I think it is wonderful to have someone care about your health so much that they drive you crazy until you do something about it.

"I learned all of this the hard way. I was not good with taking care of myself, and as a result, I was living a horrible life, going from one addiction to another. Thankfully, God kept me away from alcohol and drugs because I certainly would have become addicted to that. God taught me how to say 'yes' and 'no', and why I'm saying 'yes' and 'no' too. He kept working with me until I was able to know what my personal boundaries are and defend them with the power He gives me." I pointed to my head to indicate that knowledge is the power He gave me to accomplish this. "God provided us with this Book of Life so we can know what is the best way to live. His statutes help us to discern what is right, and He also writes statutes on our hearts so we know what He wants us to do. The ladies we are helping may not be doing things that are expressly written in the Word of God, but God has written on their heart to stop doing it. When He writes on our heart, He does not stop reminding us it is there until we act on it. That is how we know it is God. He is very tenacious."

"When did you make this board?" she asked.

"Thursday, but I had the boundaries done the Thursday before and started working them last Monday. I am in my second week, which tends to be my failure week. I keep this board in the kitchen at home so everyone who comes over sees I am trying to lose weight and exercise. Sam, my husband, can see it too and cook accordingly. He doesn't feel the need to lose weight, but he is respectful of what I am doing. He has learned a lot from me constantly having to return to eating healthy. I am praying that God will be merciful to me and continue to convict me when I eat unhealthily." We talked for a while longer about our personal struggles to do what is right, and she went downstairs just in time for Veronica to come upstairs again. This is Tabitha's new Monday habit, I guess.

Our Monday routine is to put the food away, then talk about our weekend. We both had news about our boards. "I had my first 'tweet-free' weekend in I do not know how long." I smiled.

Veronica told me about her weekend. "I am so impressed with this 'Boundary Board'. I showed it to my mother-in-law, who is a Bible-believing Christian but never talks about Jesus. She was perplexed at first when she saw it, then when I explained it to her, she was impressed with what I was doing. She knew I was working with women, but she had no idea what we were doing. She is a wonderful woman hidden with the presence of her husband so we do not have alone time very much. The odd time we are alone, we have wonderful conversations about everything. I finally felt able to tell her what I was doing and she agreed, we need to help women." Veronica was smiling. I could tell that she loves this woman dearly. "I keep my board out when it is only family, but I put it away when it is not. I am too embarrassed to let people know I am working on such an issue as negativity. I need my family to help me be more positive with them by keeping me on the right track, but friends do not need to know about this." She winked at me. "I see my desk is empty, no new clients this week?"

"Not so far, but one never knows what will happen on a bright sunny Monday," I said as I put my board in the window. We still had to take care of the clients we had, so not having any new ones left us time to work on presentations to gain new clients and have more workshops.

God decided for us that we would have Life Skills Workshops for every woman, saved or unsaved. I already had a plethora of workshops created for the unsaved. What they did not know is the information is directly from the Bible; I just did not quote it, so I am rewriting those workshops to include the Bible verses and use Jesus' name much more. I am working on that daily to be prepared. I remember the first six-week workshop I taught, called "Leading Yourself to Success". It was my first experience with teaching life skills to women. I enjoyed it immensely. God gave me the words to speak and the knowledge to answer questions. We talked about boundaries then, but I still had a lot to learn about them. Every session I created and taught, the Lord refined my knowledge of them. It was a painful journey, but it was worth every tear to be able to teach women today how to live a better, more abundant life. I expect that He is going to refine the knowledge He wants me to relay for new workshops too. He is definitely not finished with me yet.

We spent the week tweaking the workshops and praying for an avenue to teach them. We assisted our current clients with their life skills and prayed for them to understand and get revelation from God regarding their next step. We prayed for the members of our current workshop, "The White Picket Fence", to also get revelation from God this week to see His greater plan for them. God is doing a great work in all of the women who are coming to us, but He is also doing a great work in us. Our friendship is blossoming into more than I could imagine. Veronica has a great love for Jesus and our work. She gets very excited to see someone succeed, matched only by my own excitement.

Thursday was upon us, and we were super excited to see how the women made out with their first "Boundary Boards". We knew how ours were helping us, and we prayed it was functional for them too. When we went downstairs to set up, Tabitha was there. She had already arranged the tables for us and was sitting at one. The "Frappe Mocha Smoka Machine" was running, and a regular pot of coffee was brewing. I looked around with a puzzled look on my face. "This is how you set up the tables, right?" Tabitha questioned because of the puzzled look on my face. "Yes, and thank you for setting them up for us," I said.

"I bought a coffee, coffee machine because I know you are eliminating sweets from your diet for six days a week. Drinking that sugary stuff is not good for your teeth, either." She smiled at me, knowing that was not my issue. I typically brush my teeth three times a day so there is no sugar stuck on them.

"Do you think your clients would mind if I stayed here to listen?" Tabitha asked.

"I am pretty sure they will not because they just love your office and expressed a want to meet who works here. We will ask them when they come if it is okay." I said without hesitating. I ran my coffee, coffee pot back upstairs and came back down with my own "Boundary Board", which I had forgotten. See, I believe God had a hand in that, or I would have had to run upstairs during our workshop. Not every interruption is a bad one.

The ladies started pouring in one at a time until they were all in attendance. There was much chatter among them. We introduced them to Tabitha as the owner of the office. They were so thrilled to be able to tell her how much they loved the office. They have had a wonderful time in this office, and of course, enjoyed the sugarness that blurb blurbs out of that machine. They were more than happy to allow her to stay. They even pulled the other table up so she could sit with them. Tabitha's cheeks were red. Soon, she was laughing and smiling right along with them like she had been in the group from the beginning.

"Ladies." I had to say it loud enough to get their attention. A new girl in the room causes a bit of a ruckus. "Get out your boards because it is 'Week 6 - Promise Week'. Remember back in week four I asked you to pray about a verse that will speak to your promise word from Jesus. This week, I want you to write your verse out on a piece of Bristol board from this basket, and put it below your 'White Picket Fence'."

"Some of you may have already been able to get closer to your promised word on your 'Boundary Board', but all of you are getting closer to your promise by participating in this work. Success depends on many things, whether you will see significant success in one week or not. Every success is worth fighting for, because the reward is worth having. Do not get discouraged. I discovered this verse when I asked God, "Why me?" 2 Corinthians 1:3-4: *Blessed be the God and Father of our Lord Jesus Christ, the Father of mercies and God of all comfort, who comforts us in all our tribulation, that we may be able to comfort those who are in any trouble, with the comfort with which we ourselves are comforted by God.* Obviously, this verse has come into fruition for me, because as I struggled to learn how to set boundaries, I developed a better way to be successful, and that is what you are doing. God comforted me while I was going through each painful step so I could be of more comfort to you while you go through each and every painful step." Every time I refer women to this verse, it brings up painful memories, then mostly compassion for them. I feel like I am going to cry, so I had better move on.

"We know that Jesus convicts us of our sin so we will not become its slave and suffer a spiritual death. James 1:14-15 tells us: *But each one is tempted when he is drawn away by his own desires and enticed. Then, when desire has conceived, it gives birth to sin; and sin, when it is full-grown, brings forth death.* Veronica and I cannot stress enough that Christians pay a heavy price for unrepentant sin." My frown showed them how serious I am about the topic of sin. "This week, you are going to seek your own encouragement, as well as inspire each other to also seek encouragement from the Word of God."

I bought a fruit tray for the group to nibble on while discussing our boards on this, our last week of "Overcomer Training". I went to the fridge to get it, as well as the toothpicks, put it in the middle of the table, and asked Mary to begin.

"As everyone knows, I was perplexed about why Jesus was asking me to stop hugging and touching people. After five weeks of reading about it from my journal and pondering it, God revealed to me I am replacing the love missing in my marriage with love from others; it is not sexual, it is a feeling. I am not feeling loved by my husband, so I try to take it from everyone else. Jesus was right to stop me from doing that. My husband and I read the books you gave us, and we discovered he did not feel loved either. Jesus wants us to have a good marriage and we honestly thought we did, but we were deceiving ourselves. I did my journaling, studied my fence, and chose a verse to help me work through all the things Jesus wants me to stop doing. I had no idea how hard this would be." She looked down at her board in shame but looked up after reading the verse, with a smile on her face. She will be successful doing the will of the Father.

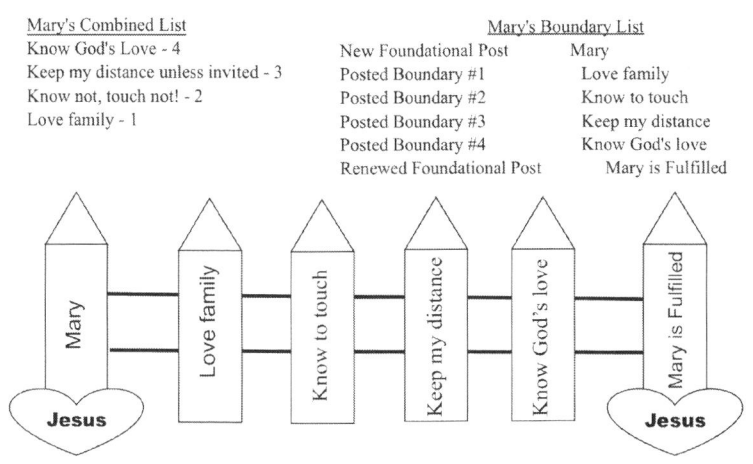

Mary's Combined List
Know God's Love - 4
Keep my distance unless invited - 3
Know not, touch not! - 2
Love family - 1

Mary's Boundary List
New Foundational Post — Mary
Posted Boundary #1 — Love family
Posted Boundary #2 — Know to touch
Posted Boundary #3 — Keep my distance
Posted Boundary #4 — Know God's love
Renewed Foundational Post — Mary is Fulfilled

And this is the confidence that we have toward him, that if we ask anything according to his will he hears us. And if we know that he hears us in whatever we ask, we know that we have the requests that we have asked of him. 1 John 5:14-15

We looked at her completed board with her verse at the bottom. We gave her a round of applause, because we all know how hard it was to come to that conclusion. She definitely has struggled with more than just anti-touching.

Nicole went next, because I could tell she was itching to talk. "I started this whole thing with the mindset that it would not work. I have tried so many ways to quit smoking but could not, because I did not know what the root cause was for my smoking. I did not need to know why God required me to quit, because I know smoking is not healthy. I wrote out my journal reluctantly but got excited about it after a couple of days. I do not like charting, so I did have a bit of difficulty figuring out what chart did what, but once I knew, I could easily create my boundaries. I can tell you my husband is on board with this all the way." She smiled in an attempt to hold back tears, but I saw a tear come down anyway. She wiped the tear away and continued. "This board has allowed me to see what I need to do on a daily basis so I have no reason to do anything else than what is written here. I read this before I leave the house each day so I know what I am facing. As you know, I love my smart phone, so I took a picture of my 'Boundary Board' and use it as my background to also remind me of my boundaries." She showed us her phone. "I also want to tell you that I have made it a habit every morning to pray for myself and for all of you too. I want to be successful and I want you to be successful too. I want my verse to be your verse so nothing dominates us besides Jesus."

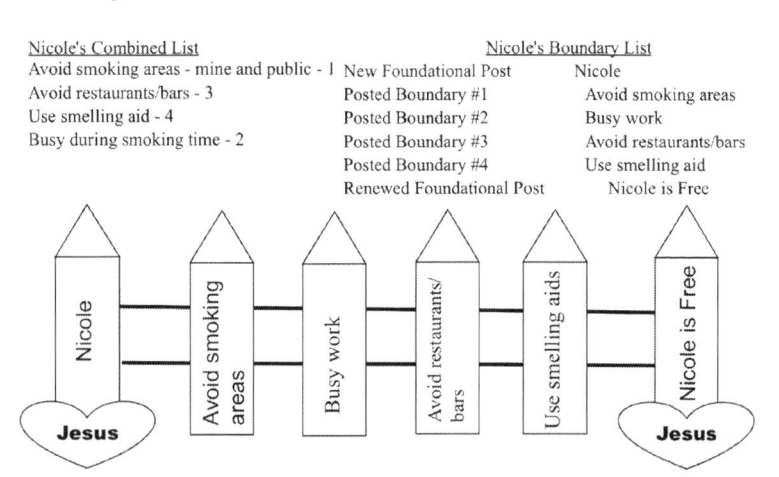

Nicole's Combined List	Nicole's Boundary List	
Avoid smoking areas - mine and public - 1	New Foundational Post	Nicole
Avoid restaurants/bars - 3	Posted Boundary #1	Avoid smoking areas
Use smelling aid - 4	Posted Boundary #2	Busy work
Busy during smoking time - 2	Posted Boundary #3	Avoid restaurants/bars
	Posted Boundary #4	Use smelling aid
	Renewed Foundational Post	Nicole is Free

All things are lawful for me, but not all things are helpful. All things are lawful for me, but I will not be dominated by anything. 1 Corinthians 6:12

Everyone examined Nicole's "Boundary Board" and

read her verse. Tabitha touched her board as if it really did not exist. She read Nicole's verse and told us she really did not know the Bible said stuff like that. I told her Paul was a guy who testified about what he was thinking, so the churches he was writing to would know he was not suffering from anything different from them. Paul was a man who wrote about what he knew, because it was his testimony.

Dory went next. "I will tell you the truth; I discovered a change in myself right away. God had convicted me to stop talking, especially about people. He knew exactly what He was doing when He brought these ladies into this neighbourhood." She looked at Tabitha for confirmation and got it; Tabitha nodded her head.

"I have needed this for years but had no way of getting it until now. I prayed about my boundaries and what they should be based on the millions of things I have said to offend people, but God told me to forget about the past and look to the future. I did feel like I needed to apologize to everyone in the neighbourhood, and I am almost finished with that. My first apology was to Leola and Veronica. God knew they would lavish me with love, affording me the encouragement I needed to make the rest of my apologies. It is in His great wisdom that I am here today. My verse was a surprise to me, because I did not even know God cared about my confidence, let alone that He wants to be it. How wonderful is that for me to know? My "Boundary Board" reflects my most dire things I need to change, so I am expecting it will take me a decade to even remove the first post."

She laughed, and so did everyone else. We all know the feeling. "If you see all of my posts, you will understand. Do you know what? I am going to have these posts put into a picture frame and hang them in my bedroom. I know this is going to be a lifetime struggle for me, so I think I will have this up on my wall for a lifetime. I want to thank you so much for loving me the way you have throughout these six weeks since you have been here. I have grown so much out of it." She came to hug Veronica and I as everyone looked at her "Boundary Board". They were nodding their heads with agreement.

All of them are lifetime boundaries.

All of us spend a little time examining Dory's "Boundary Board", because we all truly believe that what she has created is more like a "Lifetime Boundary Board", so we all agreed she should frame it. Some of the women got their journals out and wrote down Dory's words so they could use them later. For someone who thought we were deceiving her, she sure stepped up to the plate doing what we asked her to do and hit a real home run. We are extremely proud to know her and to be able to spend more time with her. It has been an honour for us much more than her.

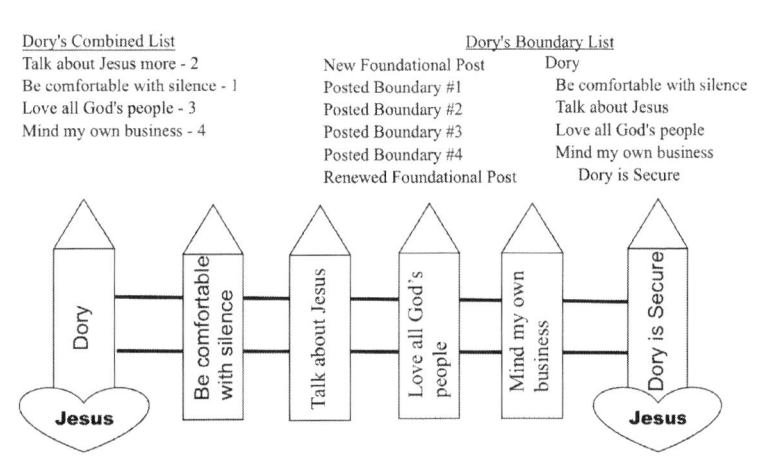

Dory's Combined List
Talk about Jesus more - 2
Be comfortable with silence - 1
Love all God's people - 3
Mind my own business - 4

New Foundational Post
Posted Boundary #1
Posted Boundary #2
Posted Boundary #3
Posted Boundary #4
Renewed Foundational Post

Dory's Boundary List
Dory
Be comfortable with silence
Talk about Jesus
Love all God's people
Mind my own business
Dory is Secure

Jesus — Dory — Be comfortable with silence — Talk about Jesus — Love all God's people — Mind my own business — Dory is Secure — Jesus

For the LORD will be your confidence And will keep your foot from being caught. Proverbs 3:26

Gladys told us about her board next. "I too want to hug both of you before I get started, because I have not shopped in seven whole days. That, my darlings, is a miracle from God." We all clapped while we hugged. "For me, it turned out not to be about the shopping. I was shopping because I was missing something in my life. I still do not know what that is but I am searching for what is missing rather than adding material things to my life. My search will most likely bring me to a knowledge of why God created me, or more so, why He chose me for Salvation. I have been asking this question for many years without ever finding the answer. I think it is time I found out what He wants me to do to serve Him. I still have the desire to mindlessly shop, unfortunately; I am required to shop for necessary items, but I have it all covered by this 'Boundary Board'."

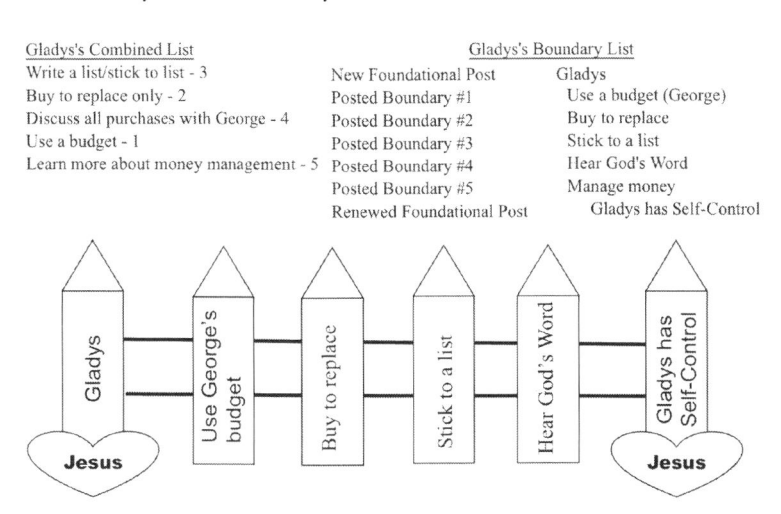

Gladys's Combined List		Gladys's Boundary List
Write a list/stick to list - 3	New Foundational Post	Gladys
Buy to replace only - 2	Posted Boundary #1	Use a budget (George)
Discuss all purchases with George - 4	Posted Boundary #2	Buy to replace
Use a budget - 1	Posted Boundary #3	Stick to a list
Learn more about money management - 5	Posted Boundary #4	Hear God's Word
	Posted Boundary #5	Manage money
	Renewed Foundational Post	Gladys has Self-Control

[Picket fence diagram with hearts labeled "Jesus" at each end, and fence posts labeled left to right: Gladys, Use George's budget, Buy to replace, Stick to a list, Hear God's Word, Gladys has Self-Control]

Wealth gained by dishonesty will be diminished, But he who gathers by labor will increase. Proverbs 13:11

"My verse is good for me because my wealth is not my own. It belongs to my husband, and I know we are one, but I am the dishonest one. I claimed his wealth without working for it. I never helped him gather, and for that, I am truly sorry. I need a reminder that the money I am spending I did not gather for myself; I am diminishing my husband. God is doing a great work in me with this one. I would never have admitted this if it were not for this workshop, because I would never have looked at myself deep enough to actually find Jesus digging around down there. Thank you so much. I am grateful to be able to become an honest wife." We hugged again. "By the way, can everyone come to my house for lunch next Thursday?" Everyone, including Tabitha, was able.

Just one woman left. I am not sure I have any tears left, but I might find two. Dee was sitting quietly. I waited to see what she would do, but she just smiled. I was touched by her smile because she looked me straight in the eyes. I know she is a changed woman.

"When Leola told me that I was being driven by my sense of taste I began to ponder that idea. Eating desserts makes me feel satisfied. Armed with this information, I began to doubt that God could satisfy me in the physical way desserts can, and that is when I truly discovered that they were indeed my idol. I was worshipping sweets and Jesus at

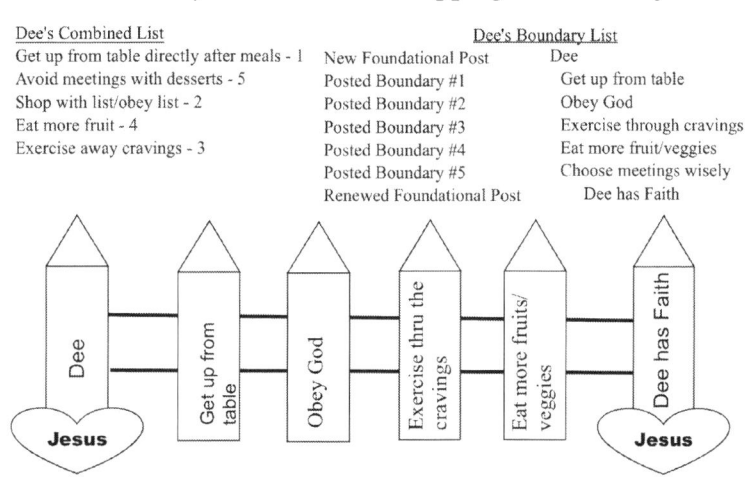

Dee's Combined List		Dee's Boundary List
Get up from table directly after meals - 1	New Foundational Post	Dee
Avoid meetings with desserts - 5	Posted Boundary #1	Get up from table
Shop with list/obey list - 2	Posted Boundary #2	Obey God
Eat more fruit - 4	Posted Boundary #3	Exercise through cravings
Exercise away cravings - 3	Posted Boundary #4	Eat more fruit/veggies
	Posted Boundary #5	Choose meetings wisely
	Renewed Foundational Post	Dee has Faith

[Fence diagram: Jesus — Dee — Get up from table — Obey God — Exercise thru the cravings — Eat more fruits/veggies — Dee has Faith — Jesus]

But whoever has doubts is condemned if he eats, because the eating is not from faith. For whatever does not proceed from faith is sin. Romans 14:23

the same time. Jesus will have no other idols before Him.[24] Having faith in the satisfaction that Jesus can provide in my life is more important to me than the satisfaction I get from eating sweets. I do not want to be condemned when I eat sweets because I lack faith[25] in Jesus Christ alone. God has transformed my mindset."

---

[24] Exodus 20:2
[25] Romans 14:23

I admired Dee's "Boundary Board" and noticed something. "Dee, did you change your picture?"

"I did, because I was not smiling in the other one. I find I am smiling more now, so I thought I needed to smile my way through being faithful to God. Do you like it?" She asked with confidence. Much more confidence than I have heard from her since we began our relationship.

"I do. You look beautiful with a smile." I said with great confidence too.

She hugged me and sat down. I advised, "This is our last week together, unless you attend the Bible Study we are planning for Thursday nights here in this office. I am very proud of you women for taking on this assignment from God and doing the work that needs to be done to overcome. He is a loving God but not easy on disobedience. It is not easy for a Christian to sin because the consequences are deadly. I want to thank you so much for allowing us to work this out with you. We have been honoured to be a part of your life."

Veronica stood up to add, "It has been a great learning experience for me walking through this with you. Although I have spent my life helping people, I have never helped anyone with a program I have been responsible for designing, as well as teaching. Leola has been doing this for a long time, so she knows what works because she has applied all of these programs to herself first. I would like to thank Leola for documenting what God has mandated her to do so she can use it to teach us." They all clapped, and I felt justified for the hard work and long hours I have put in to teach what works. I bowed my head slightly, then told them to stop before I am unable to fit my head through the door.

We sat talking to each other, as if we could not get enough of each other. There is nothing better than to be with people who have walked the same walk as you and been successful. We know it was Jesus Christ who brought us together, and we also know His plan for us may not include each other after this day. We may continue to see some of these women, and one day we may not see them again. No matter what our future entails, we know we impacted each other significantly for the time we were together.

8
THE POWER OF CHANGE

Thankfully, Gladys has made arrangements for us to meet without the workshop in the way of our camaraderie. God has completely blessed us by allowing us to teach these women. They have been open to everything we have asked them to do, even though it has hurt their pride. I am most impressed with Dory. She has stepped up in our group, but mostly in the neighbourhood. I have seen her talking with all of the neighbours one at a time. She has been much happier too. When she stops by, it is to see how we are doing and how our business is going. All of our neighbours except the folks downstairs have not been to see us in a while. We questioned their absence and chalked it up to our business. We have been doing a booming business lately. Every day, we are either going someplace to teach or have appointments with new clients or existing clients. Veronica and I are busy, yet filled with joy. We could not have asked for a better place to do our vocation, or better people to work with.

    On our very last session, Gladys invited us to lunch at her house. We accepted her invitation and scheduled it for Thursday at 12:30p.m. She told us it would be about two hours, so we planned for it. We are beginning the Thursday night women's Bible Study called "Precepts and Promises", which we invited these women to attend, and some of our other clients as well. As a result, I am spending a lot of time writing and studying the Bible. This is my forte, and I love it. I typically spend forty to fifty hours studying for one Bible study. I have to be in the secret place[26] with Jesus to understand exactly what He wants me to write. My desk is located in the perfect place for that. God speaks to me while I stare out the window, thinking about His precepts. In my days of study, I have discovered so many precepts and so many promises, we could study them until the day He takes us home and still not have studied them all. For as long as I live, I will teach this study, and as long as one woman shows up, I will show up.

    We are in our third month of helping women. In the last two months we have been shown by God how important it is to serve His people and how much they need to know from our experiences. We believe that serving His women will have a ripple effect on their whole family at one time or another. We know this because setting boundaries for ourselves has affected our families. My daughter is watching me become a woman she can rely on and a woman she can emulate. She sees me as one who stands for what I believe while loving everyone. I am doing what God wants me to do, and she is watching. Veronica is in the same situation with her two daughters. They are watching her become a woman of integrity who loves Jesus, and loves His children too. Serving Him while serving His women is forever changing our lives. God has given us what our future will look like, and we are very excited to get there, but we also know we have a long way to go to get ready for it. We are growing Christians, just like the women we serve. We know Jesus is the one changing hearts, and we are just His instruments to plant the seeds He will grow.

---

[26] Psalm 61:1 He who dwells in the secret place of the Most High shall abide under the shadow of the Almighty.

We are getting our materials ready for the church group we teach on Friday mornings, because we made the decision not to return to the office after our luncheon at Gladys' house. The women at the church are at the same pivotal point as Gladys, Dory, Nicole, Dee, and Mary were when we brought them together. We have seen one third of the churchwomen drop out for one reason or another. We definitely understand why they could not continue to do it. It is hard work setting up and defending boundaries, and unless we are ready to make the change, it will not happen. I would rather see them drop out than come and not do the work. That is very discouraging for those who are doing the work.

We are very proud of, and continue to encourage, the women who have stayed. Sometimes the reward for their hard work is not visible right away, but the reward for obeying God is almost instant. He gives us peace for our faith and obedience. The peace of God is not understood by the people around us, and sometimes not even by us until He takes it away[27] because of disobedience. Then you know you already had the reward for your obedience, the peace of God guarding your heart and mind.[28]

The women who are in the group at their church are doing quite well too, even though they already know each other. Sometimes it is easier to go through this process, or any process, with people you do not know, because we do not have to wear our plastic face. Our plastic face is the face we wear to show people we are perfectly fine, even though we are not. A lot of us wear that face to church each Sunday. I wore mine, as I am sure most women do at work and church. Mine had a fake smile and a fake look of concern for people, but I do not wear it anymore because my smile is

---

[27] Luke 8:18 Therefore take heed to what you hear. For whoever has, to him more will be given; and whoever does not have, even what he seems to have will be taken from Him.

[28] Philippians 4:7 And the peace of God which surpasses all understanding, will guard your hearts and minds through Jesus Christ.

from Jesus and for Him. When my heart is broken, it is because one of His children has a broken heart. When I hate something, it is because He hates it. I cry when He cries, and I laugh when He laughs. My face looks just like His.

I was praying for the women we are about to have lunch with when we pulled into the driveway our GPS instructed us to turn into. Gladys has lived in Russel Woods with her husband for over thirty years. They live on Russell Woods Drive in a house large enough to support every woman in our group and their families. As we drove through the gate into the driveway, both of us said, "Wow." On the left side of the driveway there were bushes and trees concealing a full size tennis court, almost the full length of the house. When we were close to the house, we saw many cars parked on the other side of the bushes, including my husband Sam's Jeep. Veronica pointed out Andrew's car too. We looked at each other quizzically and shrugged our shoulders.

We parked the car and walked up to the front door. It was a long walk past the four-car garage they have. We knew Gladys had money, but this is more money than money. The doorbell sang out, and Gladys answered the door.

"We have been waiting for you to arrive." We saw whom 'we' was when we stepped inside the door. The 'we' included all of the neighbours we have relationships with and all of our clients who participated in our first "Biblical Boundaries Workshop". We saw our husbands, plus many other men we did not know. Introductions began as Gladys shuffled us to the dining room. To my amazement, there was a table with a seating capacity of twenty in the dining room, so there was plenty of room. Gladys seated us all, putting Veronica and I at the head of the table with our husbands beside each of us. Everyone else was seated along the sides because at the other end was a beautiful tabletop hand carved lectern with Romans 8:28 written on it. Since I know exactly what that verse says, I do not have to look it up: *For all things work out to the good for those who love God and are the called to His purpose.* This is a message that rings true for Gladys now.

Once everyone was seated, Gladys got up and stood in front of the lectern with her husband George. Veronica and I looked at each other and again shrugged our shoulders. Gladys spoke first. "I planned this luncheon to thank you, Leola and Veronica, for everything you have done for me. We know that our Jesus put all this in place and is working all of it out for the good, but I want to thank you for doing what God has asked you to do. If you had not been obedient to Him, I would not have learned to be obedient to Him either, and for that, I thank you. We women are not here to thank you today, because we used our last session to do just that. This forum is not for us, but for the men. They all would like to say something too." Again, we shrugged. "My husband wanted to thank you and wanted to see if all of the men were feeling the same way, so we called every single one of them and they all agreed, so here we are." She smiled a big bright smile. All of this was unexpected and both of us are crying already. Gladys must have expected crying, because there was a box of tissue in front of each person.

George moved in front of the lectern, rustled some papers, and said, "I do not need these notes. Gladys and I have been married for forty years this year, and the best anniversary gift she has ever given me was to sign up for your classes. She was very active in the church up until ten years ago. Someone she was working with on a project hurt her feelings so deeply that she stopped all volunteer work. I have done what I could to help her, but it was not helping. The person who hurt her apologized and she forgave them, but for fear it might happen again, she has stopped doing what God has asked her to do. Her volunteer work was replaced by shopping to get out of the house. You know by now it was not the shopping that was the problem; it was the boredom. Her attitude has completely changed since she started with this group, and I am grateful for what you have done for her." Gladys was smiling from ear to ear. "I have never seen her so happy. She has peace and contentment that not even I had until she started teaching me about what she is doing. I started paying closer attention to what I was doing too, and directed it toward the common goals we have had for years but were never able to accomplish. One of those goals was to find a ministry that both of us believe in and support them financially for as long as we live. Leola and Veronica, your ministry is that ministry. We want to endow you with the first donation toward working with those who cannot afford your services with a gift of $100,000, plus our accountant/business manager will be at your disposal for anything you need done, starting yesterday. Thank you so much for what you have done with my Gladys, and ultimately me." He grabbed Gladys and hugged her close. It was obvious he loves her deeply.

    I got up and ran over to George to hug him and Gladys. This is way more than we could have ever asked for. I looked at Bert and Dory to see them shaking their heads. They had told them what our plan was with helping any woman who comes, whether they could afford it or not. We currently have three clients receiving our "overcomer training" at no cost. This money will guarantee we are able to pay our rent every month for a very long time.

    I went back to my seat to grab my third tissue. I do not know why I bothered to put makeup on this morning. I am sure there is not one lick of it left. Dee and her husband got up next. Dee said thank you first, but then turned it over to her husband Tom.

    "I have been telling Dee for years she should stop eating so many sweets, and she would not listen. God asked her over and over again to stop, but she had been unsuccessful until now. This has frustrated her for over a year and has caused havoc in our house too. I want to thank you for teaching her about herself and how to beat this habit she has. Since she has been working with you, she has become a woman of God. Dee has fallen in love with Jesus so much it has rubbed off on me. Over the last month, we have been reading the Bible together and discussing verses. She has learned through your teachings how to better apply verses to her life. We discuss them more with regards to how they affect each of us individually, and as one in our marriage. Our marriage has always been rocky because we were both self-serving. She learned in this class to submit to God, even when she did not understand what He was doing, and she began to submit to me too, with God's leading. She has changed me with her actions, and I want to thank you for everything you have done for both my wife and our marriage. Keep up the work, and if you ever need any automotive repairs done, I will do it for you for no charge at my garage." When he finished speaking, I got up and hugged them too. I am so happy God has done so much to change them. I know about living with a rocky marriage, and I also know what happens when we submit to God and each other. Amazing things will happen for them, and I am excited for them. I need another tissue. This time, Veronica was behind me waiting to hug them too. She is typically not a hugger because she is more of an introvert than I am. I hug everyone.

By the time I got back to my seat, Mary and her husband Bill were standing up. Mary blew us a kiss and Bill talked. "Mary is very gregarious and has offended a lot of people when she invaded their space, but she ignored that because she needed to feel loved. When you found this out, Leola gave a book to Mary that she had used with her husband Sam. First Mary read it, then I did. For three weeks we have purposely set boundaries around what we can and cannot do. I am not a "touchy feely" kind of guy, so my wife had been feeling unloved by me. I have begun making her feel loved by hugging her, kissing her, and generally just touching her more, and she has changed the way she talks to me by telling me how much she appreciates the things I do. I had no idea how our marriage would change just by her going for help to eliminate invading someone else's boundaries. We had no idea we did not have our own boundaries, let alone that we can have them and live better. I will be forever grateful to you for the way you trained my wife about boundaries, but more so that you cared deeply about her whole life too. Thank you so much. If you would like any help with fundraisers or anything, you need just call us. My job as a salesperson for a large automotive company affords me lots of name-dropping clients who could help." Again, we jumped up for hugs. We are so blessed to have had such a wonderful group of women for our first "Overcomer Training Workshop". It also amazed me how well they bonded to each other instantly. This is the finger of God for sure.

 It was Mark and Nicole's turn. Nicole winked and let Mark speak. "I am a non-smoker who has always hated the smell of cigarette smoke. Nicole does not smoke in the house, but it still blows in when she is smoking outside on the porch or deck. I have seen her attempt to quit so many times; I would even get frustrated for her when she started up again. She typically quits cold turkey and goes about her life as normal, then in no time, she would be smoking again, to both of our chagrin. This time she is quitting slowly by eliminating her trigger areas. At our house, it is the porch and the deck, unfortunately, but we will get over that soon enough and begin enjoying them again. I went out, at her request, to remove any ashtrays and power wash the walls and furniture. The smell of smoke is gone but the urge is still there, so she does not use them, but we know that she will be successful and we will use them again someday. We have a good marriage made better by what she has learned, and I will support her until this habit is completely eliminated. We are both positive about this. We have both decided to use our extra money from her smoking and my coffee to buy our own house instead of renting. With both of us saving, we will have a good down payment to buy our dream home when our family starts. Wink, Wink." All of us women screamed. Everyone got out of their seats for hugs this time, and the men for a shake and a hug. What wonderful news for all of us to hear. She is due next spring, so that gives them plenty of time to save for that house. How wonderful.

 Gladys calmed us all down to keep going because the caterer was coming in fifteen minutes. Bert, our landlord, was next to speak, but surprisingly enough, Dory and all our neighbours stood at the same time. Bert must be the spokesperson. "When you first came to the office to see it, I could tell you fell in love with it, but I was more interested in the money than your ministry. Another person from Toronto wanted to come and rent it for double what we were asking because he wanted the neighbourhood as clients for his financial business. Even though I felt God warning me about his integrity, I was considering him as a renter. When I tried to contact him, the phone kept cutting out and hanging up, so I could never get a hold of him, and I am forever grateful to God for intervening on your behalf. I swear He moved your name and number around the house and put it on the table in front of me everywhere I sat." Dory winked. "That was the best decision I have ever made in my life, because I have my wonderful Dory back. Over the years, Dory had become increasingly bitter and began to gossip, alienating both our families and ALL of our friends. I knew there was something wrong, but I could not get an answer out of her. I know it was very hard for her to admit that she felt inferior to everyone she knew. She got so caught up in her gossip that she was sure it was about their sin and not her own. Now that she knows, she has gone to everyone God tells her to go to and apologized for her bad behaviour. It was not easy for her to do, but she has done everything God has told her to do. You taught her how to figure out the truth about herself, and I am very grateful for that. The neighbourhood is grateful for that." They all laughed and started to clap. "The Dory I have now is the old Dory with some new spunk. She is petitioning God all the time now to tell her what to do next. She does not make a move without Him. We have been praying about what to do to thank you for all of your work and your love toward Dory, even though you knew what she was doing to the neighbours. We are going on a Caribbean Cruise in February, and we would like both of you with Sam and Andrew to join us. Everything included. Your husbands have already agreed to come, so now it is up to you."

I looked at Sam for confirmation and screamed. "Yes. Yes. Yes. Going on a cruise is on my bucket list, but I thought it would be forever before I went on a cruise because Sam has never wanted to go." I was banging my feet up and down under the table like a wild child when I saw Margaret Thatcher's master, Henry, step forward to the lectern.

"I want to say something about Dory, too. I was going to let Bert do all the talking but something inside me has been telling me to talk." He looked around and saw all of us nodding as if we knew exactly what was inside of him. "Dory has been a pain in my blank. Every time she talked to me she told the truth, but I was not ready to hear it. She told me I drink too much, then she told me I was replacing my wife with Marg. She told me I did not grieve and I am going to get sick if I do not. She is a busybody, but she was right. I was drinking too much, even for my own liking. I did get Marg because I lost my wife and could not stand to live in the house alone. I was not grieving, and my anger at Dory was keeping me going for a long time. Then she walked right up to me, looked me in the eye, and said she was sorry for her rudeness, and what I do is none of her business. I looked at her, stunned, and went back into the house. She didn't wait for me to accept her apology, she just left. I stared out the window for a few minutes, watching her putz in the garden like nothing had just happened. Then I broke down. Dory and my wife had been very good friends, so she had lost a friend too. I had not considered that she actually cared about what happened to me either. I spent the next couple of days crying for the loss of my wife and feeling sorry for Dory, who also lost a friend." We all wiped our eyes. Henry continued, "I want to thank you for loving Dory so well that she heard God speaking to her. The whole neighbourhood had stopped talking to her, and I could tell it was killing her, but I did not really care because I was just trying to survive myself. It is because of your presence in our neighbourhood that we will be able to love this new, spunky Dory. Thank you very much, Leola and Veronica, for accepting Dory for who you knew she could be and accepting us for the same."

How could anyone listen to this and not bawl? I was bawling when the caterers rang the doorbell. Sam and I went out the back patio door. We walked around so I could gather myself together. We were amazed at the back yard. Despite the fact that they lived on Lake St. Clair, they also had a pool surrounded by printed patio stones. There was a change house furnished with beautiful wicker furniture. We walked down to the dock, hand in hand, and stood on it until we heard Veronica yell that the food was ready.

We chatted while we ate the chicken parmesan with pasta. This is one of my favourite meals, so I was in my glory. She served dessert, and I watched Dee to see if she would eat it. Tom looked at her as she refused it. Since I refused the dessert too, I took the opportunity to say what was on my heart.

"You have all been so very generous to us. It is our goal to do this work without physical reward from the people we help. To be honest, we did not even expect to be paid." Everyone laughed. "We are so grateful for your generosity and for making it possible for us to continue our work unhindered for a very long time. We love where our office is located, and we love the people who share our space with us. We have great plans for the future of Crown for Life. God is showing us the amazing things he plans to do with this business and us. We are very blessed to have met you and to be allowed to be a part of your life." I am crying again. "We will include you in our daily prayers to continue setting functional boundaries and defending them with all your heart. Your life is important to God, and His plan for you is important. I feel as if God has a plan for each of us alone, but together forever. We will always be able to talk with each other. I hope you will stay together and help each other continue to overcome. Of course, you are welcome to attend the 'Precepts and Promises Bible Study', if you want to continue to see us." I had to stop talking now, as I feared I would be overcome with emotion and not be able to say another word.

Once I was in my seat, I exchanged a knowing glance with Veronica, regarding upcoming events. We have witnessed today the power of change and it is exciting. We know that God is at work and has already begun to reveal His goals with each of these women and those yet to come.

9
YOUR TURN NOW
RAISING YOUR WHITE PICKET FENCE INSTRUCTIONS

You have now read *The White Picket Fence*'s fictional characters stories, and now it is your opportunity to create your own "White Picket Fence" using the exact tools they used to build their fences. Matthew 5:37 commands us to *let your 'Yes' be 'Yes' and 'No', 'No.' For whatever is more than these is from the evil one.* It is imperative, according to the Word of God, that we have personal boundaries in order to safeguard ourselves, as well as our relationships. The "fence" referred to in this instructional chapter is our personal boundaries i.e. The White Picket Fence.

    The "Raising Your White Picket Fence" instructional is designed to help you succeed in setting personal boundaries you can live with and be safe. It is meant to be flexible in its application, therefore I encourage you to read through the whole instruction and its tasks prior to beginning. If you feel you can skip a week or combine one week with another week, please do so. You can modify it to make it more suitable as well. You are welcome to make any changes to suit your needs. You can apply at any time to join the closed Facebook group "Raising the White Picket Fence", but the call to join in this instruction is in Week 4.

The following instructions are from the "Raising the White Picket Fence" workshop, referred to throughout this novel. There are a few supplies you will need to be successful at surrounding yourself with personal boundaries, like how the characters did in this novel. The supplies in this list are used throughout the six-week period, therefore some of them will not be needed right away.

Needed for week one:
- A personal Bible (any version, although the New King James is used in this novel)
- Bible Concordance or a software search engine
- A journal

Needed for week four:
- Coloured pencils/pens
- A white board (size of your preference, if possible magnetic)
- Picture of yourself (please smile in it so you will be encouraged)
- One sheet of white Bristol board
- Magnetic tape or sticky putty (if your white board is not magnetic)

Week 1: Awareness Week

This week, you are becoming aware of the need for the "White Picket Fence". With no fence to hold you back, you are free to roam into transgressions. whether they work for you or not. Think this week about being surrounded by a "White Picket Fence", with our Jesus Christ as its foundation, and what a comfort it would be to have that fence surrounding you. Let us start first by going to the Word of God for the hope we will need to be successful.

God says in His Word: *No temptation has overtaken you*

except such as is common to man; but God is faithful, who will not allow you to be tempted beyond what you are able, but with the temptation will also make the way of escape, that you may be able to bear it (1 Corinthians 10:1). Underline this verse in your Bible and read it at the beginning of each day, so you can allow this hope to become truth in your mind. Highlight 'common to man' to know you are not alone and the word 'make' so that you understand there will always be a way out, ALWAYS. You can and will succeed, but only if you are aware of your transgressions. James 4:17 states: *Therefore, to him who knows to do good and does not do it, to him it is sin.* If God has convicted you to make changes (do good), He has made you aware of your transgression. From this day forward your transgression is sin.

What sin has God asked you to eliminate:

Answer: _____.

You are learning this week to be aware of your actions. Document everything that affects you. No secrets, because you cannot hide from God. No one will read this except you. Look up the Hope Verse and Fear Verse to write, word for word, in your journal. Choose which one will give you the most courage to continue.

Hope Verse: 1 Corinthians 10:13   Fear Verse: James 4:17

Document everything you do during each day that leads you to your sin below your chosen verse. Rewrite your chosen verse at the beginning of each day.

Week 2: Spark Week

You are now aware of the need for a "White Picket Fence". Now, you need to determine what the sparks are that will burn down your fence. Discovering what is behind your failure to succeed will help you avoid burning your fence down out of ignorance. Your understanding of why you sin will be your power to put out the spark before the fire rages. There are two references to fire in the Bible with regards to God. The first is His judgment against those who do not do His commandments[29] and the second is His presence.[30]

You are learning this week what sparks a fire in you to sin. Continue journaling this week. Write the Hope Verse: Acts 2:3 or the Fear Verse: Isaiah 50:11 in your journal at the beginning of each day. Make a chart with three columns, the same as the chart shown below. In column one, you will document what you did. You can use as few or as many words as you need for a full understanding. In column two, you will document whom you were with and what was happening when you did what you did. In column three, you will document your feelings when you did what you did. Your feelings are very important to discover, because they can be modified given the correct information about them. Remember, knowledge is power.

What did I do?	Who was I with and what was happening?	What was I feeling?

This is Veronica's "Spark Chart", filled in as an example for your reference.

---

[29] John 15:6
[30] Acts 2:3

What did I do?	Who was I with and what was happening?	What was I feeling?
I said 'no' to my son for something I should have said 'yes' to.	A lot was going on. My husband and kids were there.	I was feeling pressured.
Told my friend her dress was ugly.	Just my friend and I. We were just talking.	Powerful to tell the truth.
Was mean to the store teller.	I waited in line too long.	Frustrated and hurried.

Week 3 - Intervention Week

You have now become aware, not only of how much this transgression has affected you every day, but also what sparks a fire under you to do it. We cannot do anything about this behaviour if we never attempt to stop it. We are going to have a two-fold intervention this week. First, you are going to attempt to intervene on your own behalf, then second, you will allow Jesus to intervene on your behalf. Isaiah 43:19 says: *Behold, I will do a new thing, Now it shall spring forth; Shall you not know it? I will even make a road in the wilderness And rivers in the desert.* Just for you.

You are learning this week to allow intervention into the behaviours that lead you into sin. Continue journaling this week with the Hope Verse: Isaiah 43:19 or the Fear Verse: Proverbs 25:28 to begin your day. Make a chart with three columns, the same as the chart shown below. In column one, you will write your attempts at change. Don't think about them, just write them and try not to do the same thing the next day. If you do, document it. In column two, document whether it worked with Y or N. In column three, document how hard it was for you to make that attempt at change with 1 being easy and 10 being hard. You will continue to journal this week as well. Again I will remind you, knowledge is power.

Attempts at change	Did it work?	Easy 1-10 Hard

Pay close attention for the intervention of Jesus this week and begin reading your Bible every day. An intervention from Jesus can look like anything that makes you feel uncomfortable, such as the sweats, stomach problems, the jitters, an instant guilty feeling, or the like. It will be personal, and it will be effective. It might take some time for you to discern that it is Jesus, but allow Him to guide you through it.

Veronica's "Intervention Chart" example:

Attempts at change	Did it work?	Easy 1-10 Hard
I said 'yes' to my son rather than 'no.'	Yes	6
I kept my opinion to myself when my friend asked about her clothes.	Yes	9

Tried not to be sharp with my husband.	No	10

Work to prepare you for Week 4:

You need to know what is on the other side of this transgression. Sit with Jesus in a quiet spot and dream about what it looks like to be free of this sin. Could freedom, peace, health, purity, patience, or love be on the other side? What is God telling you will be at the other side, waiting for you? Discover the word with Jesus, then find a positive verse to match the word to encourage you to continue past these six weeks. Use the Internet, a concordance, or ask a Christian friend for a verse to match your word. Know that God wants you to succeed with this thing, because He has brought you to it to watch you succeed.

Week 4: Wisdom Week

I believe there is wisdom and accountability in numbers. *Where two or more are gathered in His name He is present.*[31] You need Jesus more than anything else to solve these problems. Working together with other women who love Jesus and are like-minded will make you stronger. This week, apply to join the Facebook group "Raising the White Picket Fence". You may also join or start a small group of women to participate in this instruction.

Having someone to talk with who is going through the same trials you are is very comforting and allows you to have an accountability partner. I want you to be able to comfort each other as you go through this. Paul says in 2 Corinthians 1:4 that: *[the Father] comforts us in all our tribulation, that we may be able to comfort those who are in any trouble, with the comfort with which we ourselves are comforted by God.* After you join the group, please

---

[31] Matthew 18:20

participate and pay attention to the posts while doing your work. You are bound to find a woman working with the same boundary, therefore you will be able to help and encourage each other.

You are learning this week the wisdom behind knowing what makes you tick. You are still journaling, using the directives from the previous weeks. Keep the charts going if you are adding new discoveries, but if you are repeating the same thing each week, having it written once in the chart is enough.

You are going to rewrite from your journaling what you need to do to be successful in eliminating these things that lead to your transgression. On a clean sheet of paper, write a list of every transgression you have committed, from week one to week three. Below on the left is Veronica's clean sheet list of things she did from her journal.

List from Veronica's Journal	**List from Veronica's Journal**
Yelled obscenities in my car	~~Yelled obscenities in my car~~
Repeated no's	Repeated no's
Told my truth	Told my truth
Bullied someone	~~Bullied someone~~
Voiced my dislike of someone	~~Voiced my dislike of someone~~
Returned mean talk	~~Returned mean talk~~
Rolled my eyes at someone	Rolled my eyes at someone
Silent treatment	Silent treatment
	Mean talk to hurt

Once your list is done go through it to eliminate similar subjects and create a new one that speaks to the ones you've eliminated. From Veronica's list above on the left, join - yelled obscenities, bullied someone, voiced my dislike and returned mean talk - together to make "mean talk to hurt", knowing that when you do these things, you hurt someone. You can cross those joined subjects out on your list and add a new subject called "mean talk to hurt" at the bottom of the list (see the above list on the right).

Easiest to Hardest to Eliminate List

1. Repeated No's
2. Told my truth
3. Silent treatment
4. Bad body language
5. Mean talk to hurt

Number each item in the list, starting from one (being easy to eliminate) to the last one being hardest to eliminate. Rewrite the list again in order (see side list). Write every one of them, regardless of the number of subjects. Whatever it takes for you to eliminate this sin is perfectly fine with Jesus. He is more interested in the elimination of the subject, especially if He is requiring it of you. Have your list ready for week five.

Work to prepare you for Week 5:
You need to know what is on the other side of this transgression. If you have not received God's word of promise to you, pray again this week, because next week you will absolutely need His word. I chose LOVE for Veronica as her word, and the verse Luke 6:31 (*Do unto others as you would have them do unto you*) to encourage her to continue. Good luck finding your word, and if you need help with your lists or your word, please do not hesitate to post a question in the "Raising the White Picket Fence" Facebook group. There will be plenty of help from your community.

Week 5 – Fortification Week

You cannot completely protect a boundary without knowing why you have created it. A fortified boundary is created with the full knowledge of why it exists. You are going to start this week by gaining an understanding of your boundaries before you set them up in your life. Your numbered list will turn into a set of boundaries to establish for yourself. Below, I have listed five different types of boundaries you will set throughout your life from this day forward. Ponder your list of numbered boundaries to identify its boundary type. This will help you discern the magnitude of each boundary. If you need to renumber your boundaries based on this list, now is a good time to make a change.

1. *Brief Boundary*: A boundary designed to be temporary for the use of cutting something out of your life for a short period of time that will impede your success, such as a weekly social outing or extra tasks. What you will cut out is not wrong, in and of itself, it is just impeding your success at this particular goal.
2. *Blanket Boundary*: A boundary designed to surround you for life. It never goes away and never stops being applied, such as not stealing or gossiping. This boundary usually starts out slow, then picks up pace until it is applied to your life forever.
3. *Burly Boundary*: A boundary designed to help you avoid an identified desire that could lead you into sin at any time. This temptation could ruin you if it leads to sexual sin, dishonesty, drugs, alcohol, abuse, anger, or the like.
4. *Bouncing Boundary*: A boundary set today but is not utilized again until the temptation returns into your life. There may be a time when something was a heavy temptation for you (such as swearing) but is not anymore, although every so often you may need to utilize this particular boundary again.
5. *Banished Boundary*: A boundary set in the past that no longer applies to your life because you have defended it with such vigor it is no longer a temptation for you, such as smoking, drinking, stealing, gossiping, or the like.

This week, you are going to learn how to fortify yourself with boundaries, and what the result is when you protect them. You created a list from easy to hard last week. We are going to use this list to build our fence, starting with ourselves, then moving toward the promised word. You will need your Week 4 supplies to continue and your positive rewritten list.

Now you have a good understanding of the type of boundaries you are about to set. They can be rewritten into a more positive form and identified as your Personal Boundaries. For an example of how to do this, look at Veronica's list below. "Repeated No's' is now "Think before saying yes or no", because she needs to think about every decision she makes without jumping straight to NO. And on the other side, she doesn't want to say YES right away, without thinking about the consequences of that either.

Personal Boundaries

1. Think before saying yes or no
2. Hold my opinion
3. Speak in love
4. Watch body language
5. Mean talk to hurt

Keep your completed list available, because you will need it for the middle fence posts. You are now going to create your "Foundational Posts", so you will need your picture and your word.

Create the parts for your "White Picket Fence"

You will need a "New Foundational Post" and a "Renewed Foundational Post", plus as many posts as you have numbers on your list. Draw and cut from your white Bristol board as many fence posts as you need. Your foundational posts can be the same size or larger than your center posts. You also need to cut out your foundation for the "New Foundational Post" and "Renewed Foundational Post", because these posts need a firm foundation, which is Jesus. You can draw them as a square or any shape you choose. I chose a heart because He loves me. Who wouldn't want a foundation based on love? The below pictures show what to draw on the Bristol board and cut out: multiple posts and two foundations for the two "Foundational Posts". Make sure the size you create matches your board.

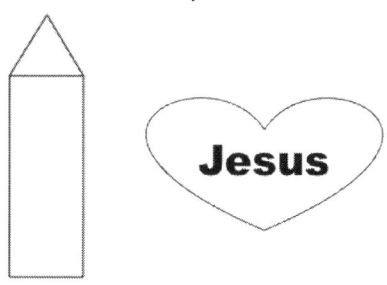

Build your White Picket Fence

Now that you have cut out your fence parts, you are going to put them together as your "White Picket Fence". *Looking unto Jesus, the author and finisher of our faith* (Hebrews 12:2a). Your foundation must be Jesus, or you will not be successful defending your boundaries. Create your "Foundational Posts" by attaching the Jesus shape to the bottom of two posts. Then, on one of the two "Foundational Posts", attach your picture. This will be your "New Foundational Post", because you are beginning anew to do what Jesus requires of you. On the "Renewed Foundational Post", write your promised word like Veronica's "Renewed Foundational Post" below, "Veronica is Love". It is called "renewed" because you are becoming renewed in your promise. Attach a magnet or sticky putty to the back of your "Foundational Posts", and affix them to your board beside each other for now, as shown below. Your goal is to move yourself toward your promise, but there is something preventing you from attaining your promise – your transgressions.

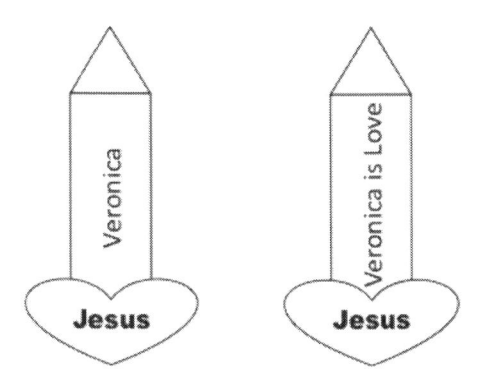

[Diagram: Two fence posts labeled "Veronica" and "Veronica is Love", each atop a heart labeled "Jesus".]

With your new list in hand, write your personal boundaries on each post. Put sticky putty on the rear of them. Starting with boundary number one beside your "New Foundational Post" (picture post), stick it to the board, and keep sticking your posts in order until you get to the "Renewed Foundational Post". The "Renewed Foundational Post" will always be your last post and remains stationary, because you are walking toward this goal it is not coming toward you. You can draw lines with a dry erase marker joining all of your posts together. See Veronica's White Picket Fence below for a visual of what your White Picket Fence will resemble.

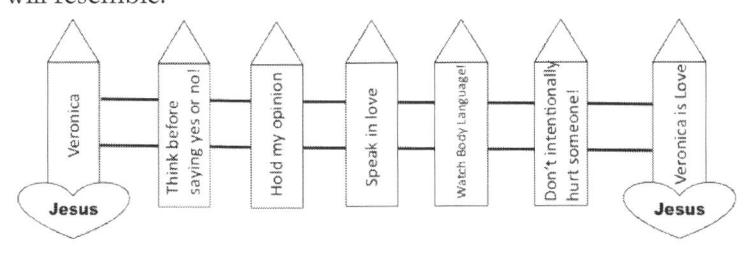

[Diagram: A white picket fence with posts labeled left to right: "Veronica" (on Jesus heart), "Think before saying yes or no!", "Hold my opinion", "Speak in love", "Watch Body Language!", "Don't intentionally hurt someone!", "Veronica is Love" (on Jesus heart).]

You have done a phenomenal job creating your board. This board is a reminder that you have established these personal boundaries in your life. Put this board in a place of prominence to remind you of each of your boundaries and the need to defend them. To inspire you to continue, you will need an encouraging promise verse to go along with your promise from God. This week, spend some time with God, as well as searching the Bible for a verse that suits your promise. I chose Luke 6:31 for Veronica's board, and I am sure you will be able to find one just as poignant. Good luck, and may the Lord be with you this week as He has been every week.

Week 6 – Promise Week

Welcome to your first week of seeking your own encouragement. You will begin to outline your own line of attack, complying with God's plan for you. You may have already been able to get closer to your promise, but you are already closer to your promise by participating in this workshop. Success depends on many things. Whether you see significant success in one week or many weeks depends on how well you are able to encourage yourself with the promises of God.

This week you are going to seek your own encouragement and inspire others to also seek their own encouragement from the Word of God. You cannot always rely on people to encourage you in person, in your small group, or on Facebook, so you will have to turn to God. Knowing the promises of God, from His Word, is the only way to get encouragement. The encouragement from God Himself can be used to support others by showing them His promises too. There are many promises in the Bible for us to seek out that will encourage us to be persistent and to help others become persistent too.

The very first promise I need you to see is that God does make promises. Peter makes this bold claim in 2 Peter 1:2-4: *Grace and peace be multiplied to you in the knowledge of God and of Jesus our Lord, as His divine power has given to us all things that pertain to life and godliness, through the knowledge of Him who called us by glory and virtue, by which have been given to us exceedingly great and precious promises, that through these you may be partakers of the divine nature, having escaped the corruption that is in the world through lust.* It is through these promises of God we can be partakers of the divine nature given to us by the Holy Spirit. The Divine nature is filled with the power we need to endure.

The next promise is most important to every one of us who profess to be Christians. *If you confess with your mouth the Lord Jesus and believe in your heart that God has raised Him from the dead, you will be saved* (Romans 10:9). This promise is as simple as that. You will be saved. You do not have to work for it nor continue praying for it – if you fulfill the directive written in this verse, you will be saved and will no longer need to wonder if you are going to Heaven – you are! Now you can relax and enjoy the rest of the promises of God.

The next promise I want you to look at is 2 Corinthians 1:3-4: *Blessed be the God and Father of our Lord Jesus Christ, the Father of mercies and God of all comfort, who comforts us in all our tribulation, that we may be able to comfort those who are in any trouble, with the comfort with which we ourselves are comforted by God.* God has comforted us all through our struggle to create these boundaries. He has been with you since before time itself. He will continue to be with you, but some women do not see or feel Him. It is our job as Christian women to comfort all women with the comfort He gives us, so they can succeed too. The best part about that is it encourages us too, and our chances to succeed will grow exponentially.

Last week, you went looking for a verse suitable for your promise. I called it the "Promise Verse" because it will be God's promise to you if you follow through on everything you have set up. Write your "Promise Verse" at the bottom of your "White Picket Fence", so when you look at the fence, you see it just like the picture below.

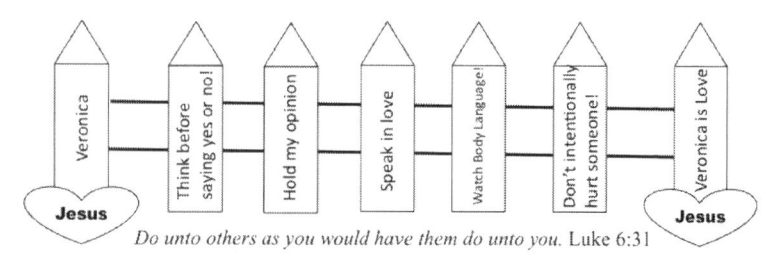

Fence diagram with pickets labeled: Veronica | Think before saying yes or no! | Hold my opinion | Speak in love | Watch Body Language! | Don't intentionally hurt someone! | Veronica is Love. Hearts at base labeled "Jesus."

Do unto others as you would have them do unto you. Luke 6:31

Read it every day until you know it by memory and it is part of your "White Picket Fence" foundation. Knowing God's promises enables us to use them to fortify every decision we make with His wisdom, not our own. Without the help of the Word of God, which is the Truth, we will surround ourselves with empty words and just as empty promises. Those empty promises will keep us weak and powerless to defend ourselves against anyone who would invade our "White Picket Fence". By raising this "White Picket Fence", you are taking the power Jesus supplies in His Word to everyone. Just as he has said: *But let your 'Yes' be 'Yes,' and your 'No,' No.' For whatever is more than these is from the evil one.*[32] You are making your "yes" be "yes" and your "no" be "no" with these personal boundaries in place.

Each time you look at or think of your board, pray for Him to burn a picture of your board into your soul and the words of your "Promise Verse". The deeper this board works its way into your soul, the stronger you will be defending every boundary you have to reach your promise. This board can be modified to use with other boundaries, or you can get an app to do it too. When your board is complete, including verse, post a picture of you smiling beside your board on the Facebook group "Raising the White Picket Fence". May God bless you as you continue to erect and defend boundaries in your life.

---

[32] Matthew 5:37

ABOUT THE AUTHOR

Kathleen V. Derbyshire has been following Jesus Christ for fifteen years. He has given her an enormous heart for women during that time. She knows the lives of these women because they are pieces of her. Kathleen and Leola are one in the same. They have the same dream to help women live the abundant life. As long as Kathleen has breath she will pray and work for women to come to know the power of Jesus and the life He wants them to live.

Kathleen has been teaching life skills workshops to women since 2005. These workshops help women establish boundaries, set goals, and find their gifts from God.

You can contact Kathleen through her website www.thelifeskillsstrategist.com and by email kathleen@thelifeskillsstrategist.com.

God has blessed Kathleen with a wonderful family, 25 years with husband Bill, along with four adult children and their spouses. Her six grandchildren are also a great joy to be with. She lives in LaSalle, Ontario, Canada, where she will continue to stare out the window to speak with Jesus.

THE PICKET WHITE FENCE

KATHLEEN DERBYSHIRE

Made in the USA
Lexington, KY
10 December 2017